THE BEST IS YET TO COME

Real Life Journey to Riches to INSPIRE You to WISDOM and WEALTH

"How CALAMITIES Can CATAPULT You to Your Divine DESTINY"

Valentina Tjan

The Best is Yet To Come

Table of Contents

Dedication	v
Acknowledgements	vii
About the Author	xi
Foreword	xiii
Prologue	xv
Chapter 1: Indonesia, My Birth Country	1
Chapter 2: Leap of Faith to U.K.	9
Chapter 3: Two Romances, One Marriage	13
Chapter 4: Newly Married Life	21
Chapter 5: New Job and New Lifestyle	23
Chapter 6: Back to U.K.	29
Chapter 7: Toronto, Here I Come	37
Chapter 8: Back to Nursing Career	39
Chapter 9: Realtor as My Third Career	51
Chapter 10: Living in the Flow of Now	63
Chapter 11: Buying Properties in USA	97
Chapter 12: Investments in Vancouver	115
Conclusion	127

To my darling daughters.

*Live, Laugh, Love, and LEARN...
forever, as long as you live.*

Acknowledgements

I first thank Raymond Aaron, who has been sending me emails advising me of what new teachings he has created each time. When the student is ready, the teacher will appear! How true it is for me!! I have been meaning to share my stories for more than 10 years! Here they are now, for all to read and apply to your own very unique situations. It is my sincere hope that my positive outlook will be able to touch some lives in an amazing way.

My sincere thanks to Liz, who reached out to me in a timely manner, which saved me hours of retyping. You must have been nudged by my guardian angel!

Thank you, Naval, for your ongoing advice and encouragement in pushing this book into being.

Sue, I am forever grateful to you for your swift and selfless help in guiding me to follow your footsteps to England.

To all my "Kesatuan" and "Regina Pacis" friends. It was very enriching to be in your company again after all these years. Keep up with as many activities as you possibly can. Thanks for including me...

To Helen, who was always there for me and enticed me to buy properties when able. You are my inspiration. Bless your heart!

I am extremely grateful to Cindy, who started as my real estate lawyer and has now become my trusted friend and confidant. You are amazing!

I definitely acknowledge my nursing unit administrator, at NICU. Had you not cut my working hours, due to the hospital's budgeting, I would still be working as a registered nurse until my retirement. I would have missed my highest and best use as an entrepreneur. Thank you, thank you, thank you!

Of course, I acknowledge all of my previous clients, who have made my career as a realtor a very satisfying endeavour.

To Grace, my long lost classmate from Grade 7 who suddenly appeared in Toronto, together with her husband, Thomas. It was ordained that you both were able to get Kevin's interest to come along to Lourdes (May 2016), the very place I wanted to visit. We both had a lovely time during those 7 days of pilgrimage. Veel bedankt, hoor!

Acknowledgements

A special thanks to Desi and her husband, who embraced us warmly by driving us to Den Haag for the whole day trip from Amsterdam.

This was one of the strange phenomena, for I had wanted to go to Den Haag when I booked this pilgrimage to Lourdes. I asked Thomas if it would have been possible, on the way back (after Lourdes), to be dropped off in Den Haag instead of Amsterdam, and he said "no." Although I just met you, Desi, during the pilgrimage to Lourdes, your hospitality was so touching! Hopefully, Kevin and I would be able to return your kindness in the near future.

To Mel in Darmstadt, West Germany: Your hospitality is greatly appreciated! Danke sehr!

To Tjays, whom I had the pleasure of reconnecting with in Melbourne. Thanks for taking the time to show me lovely places in Melbourne, Australia. Let's meet up again soon!

To Waqas, thank you for being patient with me. Your artwork is very much appreciated.

To Lisa, thank you so much for your great work in editing and formatting.

Last but not least, I extend my gratitude to my husband, Kevin, who has been my greatest teacher of all time, for 44 years. Time has indeed skyrocketed! The BEST is yet to COME!!

About the Author

Valentina lives with her husband in Toronto, Ontario, Canada. Her innate positive outlook in life is duplicatable for anyone who wishes to have a joyful, meaningful life blessed with wisdom and wealth.

Practice is the key to create that possibility, plenty of practice at all times.

She will be so happy to receive any feedback about this book, and can be reached at vtjan1@outlook.com

Foreword

Do you live your life with an attitude of gratitude? Are there things in your life that you'd like to change? If your answer to my second question is yes, then it's entirely possible that your answer to my first question is no. In order to attract abundance into your life, you need to think positively.

If you find this a difficult concept to grasp, author Valentina Tjan is the person to help you! I first met Valentina about thirteen years ago during one of my seminars, and had a strange feeling that somehow we would meet again in the future. I was thrilled, therefore, to hear that she had written *The Best is Yet to Come.*

I really love the three main concepts she discusses:

1. An attitude of gratitude is a prerequisite to sailing happily through your life.
2. The power of good intention will propel you to witness your goals unfolding beyond your wildest expectations.
3. Doing what you enjoy and utilizing your talents are your own unique gifts in this life.

The Best is Yet To Come

You hold in your hands a tool to a better life. I urge you to start reading it thoroughly today!

Raymond Aaron
New York Times Bestselling Author

Prologue

THE BEST IS YET TO COME:

This title was chosen to metaphorically state my 99% state of mind at any given time-POSITIVE, specifically when the going appears tough!

This positive thinking helps my life in leaps and bounds, as I shall present the experiences in more detail inside this book. Hopefully, my real life journey will encourage some of you to adopt the principle to always seek assets within yourselves, and to keep on expanding your own realms.

I also have had an innate constant attitude of gratitude from a very young age, as many people around me were poor, and I felt privileged amongst them. In my opinion, with this attitude, you will automatically sail on joyfully in this life, as there are plenty of people who suffer so much more in comparison.

This strengthened my positive thinking whenever I weathered the adversities, which are plentiful, too.

Believe it or not, my glass is always half-full, never half empty. Whenever the going gets tough, I reflect and pause, and then I get busy racking my brain how to find the meaning or even the potential abundance at the end of the trial. The attitude of gratitude has definitely played a large part in my life journey.

Whenever I feel helpless, I will purposely help one of my friends, whom I perceive might need some comforting words. Kindness, hopefulness, helpfulness, and all the positive factors, have always been very useful and essential for getting persistent good results in my life.

My parents were a middle-class family, with my mother being there full time for us, four children. I am the youngest and the only girl in the family, and my compassionate, patient, and philosophical father encouraged me at all times. He was indeed the best father for me. I could never do anything wrong in his eyes. This fact alone was indeed the mighty driving force for me, which shaped my personality and integrity. Fondly, I can still feel that agape/unconditional love vividly…! Plus, I was always praised for doing the right and proper things in life, by my family and my teachers in school. My confidence, without being arrogant, (plenty of things grounded/humbled me) thrived tremendously from my tender age.

I loved school and excelled throughout my school years from grades one to twelve, and persistently ranked number one. Being helpful to my classmates, especially in mathematics, gave me popularity amongst them, and also on the other hand enabled me to remember the formulas so very naturally. Hence, the win-win scenario was born very early in my mindset. This win-win philosophy was the inspiration for my real estate brokerage, which I started in 2003. I have always applied this knowledge for all my transactions and it is the BEST way. I do not have to make one side lose, in order to benefit the other side. Both sides should experience the benefit, if and when the transaction can be called successful.

Since my two daughters left home and are independently doing well financially, I now only work on repeats and referrals in my real estate business. I travel to Florida once or twice a year to see my eldest daughter and her husband, and their family, which consists of two lovely dogs and a cat.

My youngest daughter and her husband live in Vancouver, British Columbia. My husband and I travel to stay there for about a month, either once or twice a year. Fortunately, we own our comfortable and cozy homes away from home, both in Florida and Vancouver. (More about how we obtained these properties in later chapters, with the good INTENTION behind those purchases in USA and Canada.)

The Best is Yet To Come

In the next chapter, I will share a few of my surreal spiritual experiences during my growing-up years in Indonesia.

Some of the names in this book were changed for the purpose of privacy protection.

Chapter 1

Indonesia, My Birth Country

"Our greatest glory is not in never falling but in rising every time we fall." ~ Confucius

I am planning to share all the joy of being an optimist here. These testimonials of living joyfully by design have been pushing me to give birth to this book as the means to encourage people to always think positively.

My ancestors are from China, and my family has always instilled the pride of being Chinese, with the ancient philosophers, Confucius's and Lao Tzu's ideology often mentioned throughout my growing up years.

The political situation in my birth country, during my teenage years, was not ideal for Chinese. Indonesian government did not like the fact that many Chinese dominated the economy, sports and academic world. So, we needed to follow the policy, (i.e., to change our Chinese names to Indonesian names). I was in grade 11 when I had to change my Chinese surname from Tjan to Chandra; and coincidently, I was baptized in a Catholic church at the same time. My baptism name was then adopted as my first name.

To pay respect to my late father's legacy, I am using his family name, Tjan, on the cover of this book, which I also legalized after establishing my business as an entrepreneur in properties.

My mom often advised us to avoid any exclusive relationship with the opposite sex during our growing years, until at least our college years, and this idea was accepted very graciously by my 3 brothers and myself. I never wanted to have a serious relationship with any boy during grade school, as it might become a hindrance to my future career.

When I was 13, I had my first glimpse of a spiritual phenomenon: I could see vividly in my dream how to repair our newly purchased TV set that had malfunctioned the evening prior to my dream. I insisted on opening the back of the TV set, and I just tightened a few buttons as shown in my dream. Then, voila, the TV worked again! A few weeks later, I had another surreal dream, following my arithmetic test. Being in a Catholic school, I adopted a habit of saying a little prayer each night prior to my sleep. I was having quite a forlorn feeling about the little error I had made on my test that day.

So, I prayed deeply that night prior to my sleep: "Please God, creator of heaven and earth, make my teacher overlook my slight error and give me a 100% mark." That night, in my dream, I saw that my mark was 100%. I was so ecstatic about this. I got up with a smile on my face and felt confident that this dream was giving me a sneak peek for the fate of my test. It was indeed what happened. To my heightened anticipation, I received a 100% mark that day.

Through the conservative upbringing by my parents, I sailed through my teenage years blissfully. From the age of 15, I started earning some pocket money by giving private tutoring to the neighbors. I was not looking for a job at all. It so happened that my neighbors were both too busy working in their family business. They felt their children, who were just three and four years my junior, could benefit from me, since I was doing very well in school.

A few years later, when I was in grade 11, my aunt (my mom's younger sister), who lived in Holland, wrote to my mom that her husband (who was a respected MD in a large Rotterdam Hospital) knew that there was a shortage of nursing students in the hospital where he was working. He happened to be friends with the one in charge of accepting new students. Through this connection, as well as my academic credence, the hospital started a Visa application for me to enter Holland at the earliest convenience. I then started learning the Dutch language, three times a week.

Initially, when my mom asked me if I was interested in going to Holland to be trained to be a nurse, I was feeling kind of sad, "How could you ask me to leave you? Don't you love me? How could you ask me to leave all my family and friends to go to a place so far away?" She showed me the letter. In it, I read that as a trained registered nurse, the career was supposedly highly respected, and the salary was more than enough to live comfortably. Another perk of taking this offer was that during the training, the hospital would give me free board and lodging, and the monthly salary would support me to live well. This was such an incentive to know before I decided to go for it, that I would undertake something solid.

All three of my brothers needed university education, and now this was my chance to lighten my father's burden by taking this offer. Hence, after a few days, my mind was made up!!

It turned out that by making a decision for the benefit of my dad, over and above my very own, the rewards were indeed multiplied exponentially. I felt that I had been recognized and highly rewarded by God, our most loving Father, many times whenever I chose my actions/decisions for the greater good. It never escapes my attention, as you will see by reading about the things I am sharing in my very own life journey. Consequently, I always strive to do the right things in accordance with my conscience.

Although it is not such a life-changing experience when people from the outside are looking in, some of the mundane things never cease to amaze me. I always feel special when the little day-to-day occurrences guide me step-by-step. I recall some substantial incidences that cannot be explained in any other way, the ones that were obviously about the law of the Universe. When I do good things with good intentions, I will be shown results that often exceed way above my expectations.

These all must have been due to my constant communication with my spiritual guide. I strongly believe that we are all given a guardian angel to handle our day-to-day lives. We need to believe this FIRST; then we will see!!

Preparation to Fly Away

"The pessimist sees difficulty in every opportunity.
The optimist sees the opportunity in every difficulty.
Difficulties mastered are opportunities won!"
~ Winston Churchill

I felt very upbeat about my decision to go to Holland to further my study. At this time, I only had one group of 4 private students to teach twice a week. This enabled me to take Dutch language lessons, 4 times a week. I really enjoyed learning this new language. Unfortunately, my ability in speaking Dutch had disappeared almost totally, through non-use of this language for decades. Quite a pity!

This exciting anticipation gave me so many flying dreams. I would soar in the sky with ease and great enjoyment, looking down in awe at the houses, the green grass, and the flowers, and at the same time having an exhilarating feeling. These indeed assured me that everything would work out easily and smoothly. Well, not so fast, though. I graduated from high school, but the Visa to Holland was still not forthcoming, and it had been almost 1 year since the application was submitted. While waiting, I applied and got accepted at the local university, studying to be a veterinarian.

One semester flew by, and the request to have my medical check-up at last arrived. I had to go to Jakarta for this (I lived in Bogor, 60 km away from Jakarta). In the evening prior to going to Jakarta, Sam, my former classmate, paid me a visit out of the blue. He came to my house a few times when we were in the same class in grade 10. At this time, we did not date at all, as per what I mentioned before, i.e., I did not wish to be tied down with anyone until at least college years.

He left Regina Pacis, my high school, when I was in grade 11. It turned out that he was sent to Formosa by his dad, to further his study there, and we corresponded occasionally. We were just pen pals.

To my great delight, he offered to go with me to Jakarta, and I gladly accepted his company.

Our feelings of mutual attraction developed on that day, but we did not expect too much substance as we would be so far apart during the course of our study.

So, we parted ways with just some hopes that we would still write to one another, and we left it at that. We did not even hug or kiss goodbye, as both of us understood that our journey in pursuing our career is still very much uncertain.

Meanwhile, another neighbor asked if I could spare some time to teach her 2 kids, and I happily agreed. This mother, Jan, turned out to be the catalyst that sped up my going abroad, not to Holland as per my plan, but to England. One early afternoon, when I was about to teach at Jan's house, she was about to go to the airport to send Sue off to England. I asked if Sue was the one that was supposed to go to Holland to do a nursing study like myself. I had met Sue at one of the parties just 2 months earlier. Jan answered in the affirmative. I immediately gave Jan a piece of paper with my name and address on it, with a message to get Sue to write to me about how to follow her to be accepted in the hospital where she would be.

Chapter 2

Leap of Faith to U.K.

"I hear and I forget. I see and I remember. I do and I understand."
Confucius: 559 B.C. to 479 B.C.

Within 10 days, I received a letter from Sue, including an application form. That day happened to be my birthday too. I quickly filled out the application form and mailed it on the same day. On December 23rd, just six weeks after my mailing the application, I received the acceptance letter to start the training on January 4th, as well as a temporary Visa to enter England. I was very pleased that the process was so swift indeed. On December 30th, I boarded the plane to England, and arrived on December 31st, in the afternoon. A shuttle minivan picked me up and took me to an office not too far from my training hospital, where a cab was then booked on my arrival.

I felt quite calm and trusting that all would be well, since Sue would be in the same nurses' home as I was. Not long after my arrival, Sue came to my room, together with 2 other nurses, and we chatted for about 15 minutes or so, as it was 9:30 p.m. by that time. My new world, so far away from my family and friends, had begun. My English language was not good, as I did not prepare myself to converse in English, other than what I had learned from my intermediate and high school, which was not much. Sue suggested that whenever we were together, we should converse in English instead of talking in the Indonesian language. I wholeheartedly agreed to her smart suggestion.

She told me that I could join her in going to the college next door to study English as second language. This was twice a week. My days in England were so filled with activities immediately that I did not have time to feel homesick. I forced myself to write only in English to my mom and dad. For sure, I wrote to Sam, also in English.

This strategy helped me immensely to adopt the English language in no time at all. The new and definitely interesting chapter of my life began furiously fast, and yet it was such a smooth transition. I always look at it as a sign from the Higher Power, that since I put myself as an instrument for the greater good, everything just lined up neatly and pleasantly for me. I felt I could enjoy all the new things in my life, starting from the classroom activities for the first four weeks, to the practical side of nursing, (i.e., working in the wards of the hospital, nursing the sick). Considering that I was very uncomfortable with blood and dying people, looking back, I am often amazed that all the fear seemed to have vanished. It was irrelevant once I decided that my leaving Indonesia would greatly take a burden off my dad's shoulders. Over the twenty years during my nursing work, I only had to deal with two "last offices," which was the term used to wash up the dead bodies. One was when I had to assist the senior nurse, and the second was when I was the senior being assisted by a junior nurse. That time, when I found that the junior nurse was just as uptight and scared as I was, I could not help myself from laughing at the absurdities of the situation. Both of us ended up outside the room with nervous laughter, and then doubled up uproariously. The charge nurse was a real angel! She just sent us to do other things, and then went into the room by herself and did the "last office" all on her own!! That was so incredible.

She never mentioned it to anyone else. I was really spared from the uncomfortable duty without a hitch.

Another surreal spiritual intervention was when I was assigned in the heavy ward of patients with MS (multiple sclerosis). It was kind of physically and psychologically draining, as all patients were in wheelchairs, and they were very specific in their requirements of their own sequences.

The charge nurse was a very kind, caring, and observant maternal figure to everyone, including me, who in her opinion looked tired and drawn out. After only 2 weeks working there, suddenly I was placed in a male ward, with many young college/university students working during their summer vacation. That was indeed a refreshing working atmosphere to be in.

The music was often blasted rather loudly during the day; and one of the university students, Dennis, a medical student from Ireland, was very charming indeed. He often, a bit flirtatiously but charmingly , called me "Sweety Pie" or "Honey Pie," and he reminded me so much of Sam, who by that time I considered as my far away "boyfriend."

Dennis was quite amused about the fact that as a young lady (I was 19 at that time, and Dennis was 21), I did not have the inclination to date anyone else. In his opinion, the possibility of the long distance relationship was just futile. I just told him that the difference between the West and the East, as far as loyalty was concerned, was like day and night. He said playfully that if he would ask me to dance with him, I would definitely say, "Your wish is my command." To this, I quipped good naturedly, "Never, Dennis!"

I was strongly convinced that the guys with Eastern values would be just like my dad, who was a steadfastly loyal and loving family man. (Ha-ha-ha, what a thought! In the next chapters, you will know why.)

Chapter 3

Two Romances, One Marriage

"A good traveler has no fixed plans, and is not intent on arriving." Lao Tzu

After just about one year in the U.K., I managed to achieve third position in my class, and I patted myself on the back for this. The *attitude of gratitude* has always been nurtured by me, no matter what. It always serves me very well to take this stance: The BEST is yet to COME!

The only certainty for all of us is that we are all going to die, and this eventuality will definitely be the BEST outcome. This will mean that we are back to where we all come from, i.e., the spiritual world. For the ones who strive to do the right things, in accordance with our own spiritual growth, heaven above is awaiting us, and for those who decide to go the other direction ...who knows?

The main thing is to participate in this life, JOYFULLY, as you and I each are a piece of a jigsaw puzzle, interdependently forming a big picture.

Not long after this small feat, Sam wrote that he would further his study in England. This was exceptionally wonderful news for me, as we could then be together during our study, but not living together prior to our marriage. I was very much against common law living arrangements.

We saw one another on most weekends for about two years, and it was quite blissful courtship as we seemed to be quite compatible. In the third year, Sam moved to Leeds to start his first year of university, and I remained in London to finish the last year of my nursing study to become a state registered nurse, and upon passing the final exams, I would have a title of SRN behind my name. A couple of months prior to my final exams, I applied to a hospital in Leeds to do a midwifery course for 12 months, and I got accepted with a provision to have passed the SRN final exams.

Before my final SRN exams, my parents sent money for a round trip plane ticket to Indonesia, for a 5 week stay, which I accepted gratefully. I had not seen them for about 5 years by that time.

When Sam kissed me goodbye at the airport, I sensed a brief uneasy feeling that somehow he might not be able to withstand the lonely 5 weeks all by himself. But when I arrived in Bogor, his letter welcoming me was there. I found it very romantic indeed, and it consequently threw the uneasy feeling I had earlier as completely unjustified sentiments.

The five weeks in Indonesia flew by so fast, as I was treated by going to Bali and other tourist areas nearby.

Sam picked me up at London Heathrow Airport, and then brought me to a boarding house occupied by some new students from Indonesia, plus one girl from Malaysia. There was a strange incident though.

The girl that he introduced to me as his former classmate in London, was only speaking in Chinese with Sam. I thought her English must have been too limited, and that Sam was just being polite.

They seemed lost in their own world, talking in Chinese animatedly, and since my Chinese was negligible , I could not join the conversation at all. I thought nothing of it! Never in a million years would I have thought that Sam, out of his loneliness, during my 5 weeks absence, would already have started getting to know her in a way that would lead to our breakup. More about this later…

About two weeks after my return from Indonesia, I received a letter telling me that I had failed my SRN exams.

Of course, I was quite devastated by this news, but being forever hopeful, I immediately bounced back. Right away, I sent the form to do another exam in three months' time.

My midwifery training was also on hold until such time that I passed. In the meantime, the hospital employed me in the postpartum area, taking care of the newborns, plus the new mothers.

A few days down the road, when Sam and I did grocery shopping, I noticed that he was a bit distracted and impatient with me. Playfully, I just blurted out: "You seem to be very preoccupied and distant.

Just wondering if you still love me?" To my horror, his reply was: "I am not sure."

I had no news from him for 2 weeks. One Saturday, I bumped into Pam, who had been at a party Sam and I attended when I first arrived in Leeds. We seemed to like one another instantly as we have a lot in common. After chatting for a few minutes, I asked her if she would go with me to Sam's student' dormitory. I had only been there once, with my London friend the year before.

She was happy to accompany me there. When we got there, he asked us to sit in the shared kitchen with other students. I had to excuse myself to use the washroom, and after that, I felt compelled to open the door of Sam's bedroom. Surprise, surprise...the girl that had been chatting in Chinese with Sam in London was there!! I had been guided there to see this ugly reality. I remained calm and just left, feeling sick to my stomach. Pam was very understanding about this and let me vent to my heart's content. She brought me to her friends' house, and they were very kind and supportive towards me. They insisted that I should stay in their house for the night, as it was rather late for me to travel back to the nurses' home alone.

Pam lived within a short walk from their house. I gratefully accepted their exceptional hospitality. After this shocking revelation I had just experienced, I managed to sleep pretty well, to my great surprise. I prayed with all my heart that Sam would want to get back to me, and by that time, I would have found someone else. And to my delight, that was what happened. I found out about his dalliance around the end of November, and I met my future husband, Kevin, on December 31st, at an all night Indonesian party at that amazingly kindhearted couple's house. It was attraction at first sight, I would say. He invited me to join a bus tour to Blackpool, and he chose to sit next to me on the bus. After that, we started seeing one another quite regularly. As Leeds is a small town, before too long, Sam must have heard that Kevin was serious about me. My life was very busy indeed during that time, studying for my SRN exams again, plus working full time, as well. My second attempt for SRN exams was the end of January, and the results were out in March.

I passed!! What a great relief. I immediately started my midwifery course, for 12 months.

Sam wanted to get back with me in March, just 3 months after I found him cheating, caught red handed, very unexpectedly. My prayer was answered to the letter!! I learned that when there is a calamity, if I would just busy myself with other activities, I could always expect nice things to be waiting for me, and to invariably turn out better than I expected. The best thing was, my realization that I could totally surrender to my Creator in the face of calamity, to let go and let God. Hence, I would sleep very well indeed instead of losing my sleep. Basically, I could surrender when I feel overwhelmed.

Kevin, my new "knight in shining armor," had a long talk with me and told me that I should never consider going back to Sam, under any circumstances at all. The way Sam jilted me, at the same time that I had just failed my SRN final exams, and being in a new surrounding, and a new undertaking, spoke volumes about how cruel he could be. His newfound love made him totally selfish. Would I take another chance with someone with that kind of weakness?

Another very important factor that made my decision easy, (other than my prayer to be able to say "No" to him when he wanted me back), was Kevin's past experience in Singapore. He had fallen in love with one of his classmates who had just broke up with her boyfriend, and a short while later, that girl went back to her former boyfriend. How could I inflict this same pain on him, when he had been my rock when I was very vulnerable?? I just had to say goodbye to my first love. That was the only decent thing to do; besides, my love for Kevin had grown quite a bit by that time.

Subsequently, Kevin paid Sam a visit and told him that he was not welcome to see me anymore. From then on, Sam left us alone. Kevin and I were married after our graduation: he as a civil engineer, and I as a state certified midwife (SCM) specializing in the NICU (=neonatal intensive care unit), about 18 months after we met.

We had a very simple but memorable wedding reception at my medical residence, with 27 guests attending. Some of my friends from London came by to celebrate our milestone of being a married couple.

The wedding cake was made by my colleague's' husband, who worked in a German bakery. Our main focus was to have a good harmonious life together, and not to spend too much money and energy on the wedding party.

We kept a big chunk of our wedding cake in the freezer, and let our family back in Jakarta, as well as in Bogor, taste the typical Western wedding cake with rum, as to give the taste, and at the same time preserve it too.

The Best is Yet To Come

We went on our honeymoon to Italy for a week, before heading back to Indonesia via Singapore.

Kevin and I enjoyed our second honeymoon in Singapore, for a week, before launching our new careers.

Chapter 4

Newly Married Life

"He who conquers others is strong. He who conquers himself is mighty." Lao Tzu

After staying in Singapore for a few days, Kevin and I went to our birth country, Indonesia, to start our new life together. We were both very hopeful of landing a pretty good career for each one of us.

As for our residence, Kevin's mom welcomed both of us to live together in her house. She had one daughter still living with her, and the house was big enough for all of us to stay there. Kevin's dad passed away when Kevin was 9 years of age. I had great respect towards my mother in law, who had to raise her six kids single-handedly, and even managed to send her two youngest children to study in Singapore for 3 years, and then in England for another 3 years.

Soon, Kevin and I were busy every day, trying to find some work during the days, and visiting family during the evening.

We were without any work for about 3 weeks, and were enjoying all the good food that we had missed for many years during our studies abroad. My mother's neighbor asked if I could teach her son on the weekends. Her son was in grade 7. I accepted happily, with the anticipation that I would have a very valid excuse to visit my parents, from Saturday evening till Sunday afternoon, every week.

My parents were also very happy with this arrangement. The win-win outcome was indeed the result of taking such a simple undertaking!

Day-to-day life was very hectic for us, albeit interesting and harmonious! My mother's neighbor gave us a cute little puppy to add to our joy. I named this cute puppy, "Jovial."

Life was indeed wonderful!

Chapter 5

New Job and New Lifestyle

"Instead of being concerned that you were not known, seek to be worthy of being known." Confucius

I knew that I would not work in a hospital in Indonesia. The nursing profession in this country did not command much respect, and the pay was not good either. Kevin met with his former private tutor, who worked in a pretty large company that was managed by a British person. So, it was quite a good fit for him to apply to work there. He was accepted easily, since there was an insider helping the process.

The company gave him a brand new car, a Toyota Corolla, for his office-related business, and private use as well.

Kevin's brother introduced me to his childhood friend who was about to open an import-export company, which would require a secretary with a good command of the

English language. I was interviewed and got accepted, which made me feel so grateful. Given that I had been job hunting for such a relatively short time, I felt very blessed indeed.

My week was occupied by a full time job from Monday to Friday, from 9 to 5, plus Saturdays from 9 to 2 p.m. I liked this as I did not wish to stay home too much, especially because of the fact that we still lived with my mother-in- law. As the saying goes, "Familiarity breeds contempt."

I for sure would like to avoid the above saying becoming a reality for me. Prevention is always better than cure.

After about a year in this domestic bliss, my mother wanted to have a party of Thanksgiving, being that all her four children were doing well financially; and at the same time, she longed to have my marriage blessed by a priest. Kevin and I invited the wonderful couple, Nell and Ross, who were extremely kind when I was so distraught on that fateful evening of finding out the truth behind Sam's peculiar behavior. Nell even told Sam off in public about how disappointed she was with his behaviour. Certain things happen mysteriously. I am a very forgiving person; I let bygones be bygones! Life is too short to hold a grudge mercilessly. I could very well understand why it happened. We were not meant to be in one another's life, period! We were too similar, and we would not have been challenged to grow to be what we were ordained to be. At times, I still fondly reminisce about my first love, which was crushed by the fate that had strengthened my resolve and my understanding of how weak one can be in the face of temptation.

A few months went by uneventfully, and Kevin and I were so busy that time just flew by! We requested two weeks' vacation to visit my paternal aunt and uncle who live in East of Java. On the way there, we picked up my brother to join us for some family gatherings. The visit went well indeed. Kevin was the only one driving as I did not know how to drive yet, and my brother did not have a driver's license at that time. After dropping my brother off on the way home, on rainy day, the car skidded and hit another car. Other than feeling the shock, Kevin did not suffer any physical injury. I was hurt quite badly; my pelvic bones were fractured in three places, and I had to be hospitalized for five days.

I had a plaster cast from my waist to my ankles, which had to stay in place for 3 long weeks. Obviously, I had to be on bed rest for that time, and the only place suitable for me was in my parents' house, since they had one live-in servant and another one came in daily. Naturally, I also would find myself very much at ease having my beloved parents around during my bed rest period.

During those 3 weeks, Kevin stayed with me, and he had to commute over one hour, one way, to his job.

We both took things in stride, like ducks take to water. There were no complaints, and no depression ensued, I am happy to recollect.

After the plaster cast was removed, I had to relearn how to walk and move about, which seemed to be quite a challenging task, especially when I had to squat. I had to do them slowly and with such great care and focus.

Two weeks later, I felt more like my normal self and went back to work. I would be driven to the train station by Kevin, and picked up from my office by him. We would be traveling back together all the way by car to my parents' house. We had gotten used to staying in my parents' house in Bogor, 60 km away from Jakarta. It was quite a lot cooler as it is surrounded by mountains.

Both Kevin and I felt ready to start a family after just over one year of marriage. Three months went by, and we were not pregnant yet. The hectic six days of commuting to work must have been the reason for my inability to conceive, as I never took any birth control pills at all. All the time prior to our plan, I was using a natural method of contraception, such as taking a daily body temperature to find out the time that I would ovulate. I applied the natural techniques that I had learned and then taught to the patients during the 12-month-course of my midwifery training.

New Job and New Lifestyle

In my mind, I decided that I should proactively try to find another secretarial job, in a company that works from Monday to Friday only. Lo and behold, one fine afternoon, I called one company (called Natterman) and, coincidentally, they were in need of a secretary. Their present secretary was going to London, U.K. to further her study. They asked me to come for an interview, and I got the job! Another good thing about Natterman, other than Saturdays and Sundays off, is the distance.

It was only 30 km away from my parents' house, just half an hour drive, in the same direction to Jakarta.

Kevin would drive me all the way to my new office, and pick me up on his way home. Nice...

Life was good for us. Immediately after moving to Natterman, (a pharmaceutical company owned by some Germans), I was pregnant! I really wanted to deliver our baby in England, as I have a high opinion of their health care, and I also wanted to ensure that my permanent residence in the U.K. would be renewed (prior to my 2 years being away from England).

I applied to my SRN training hospital and was accepted in an eye ward as a junior charge nurse. This was perfect, as this job was light and had a pleasant atmosphere, as far as I could recall during my two years training there. By the end of July, I was back in England. Kevin stayed back at my parents' house. We needed him to keep his job and to finish building our future house in Bogor.

Chapter 6

Back to U.K.

"The cautious seldom err."
Confucius

I was very ecstatic and grateful to be back in England, although a little bit melancholic without Kevin by my side. Our plan was to migrate to Australia. We had started the application from Jakarta a few months earlier. Quite soon after my arrival in England, I went to the Australian Embassy to update my address for them to send the result of our application. After waiting for about 6 months, to my slight dismay, a rejection letter arrived. I consoled Kevin in my letter, and myself, too, that God had better plans for us.

Meanwhile, my job in that eye ward, as I predicted, was indeed very delightful and simple. No sweat at all! Before too long, I decided to tell everyone in there that I was expecting a baby. Everyone was genuinely happy for me, and even more caring and helpful, too.

Kevin and I wrote letters very frequently to one another. No cell phones, texting, or emailing was available at that time. We had to contend with letters by mail, which took at least one week to arrive. We accepted our situation matter of factly. Both of us were very occupied in our daily undertakings. Time flew by very fast. Soon came November, with the news that my husband Kevin had already booked a flight, to arrive mid-December, before Christmas!! Our baby's due date was March the 8th. Perfect timing!!

The house he built for us was ready, and he had to pay someone to be the care-taker.

Although very fleetingly, I was wondering how we were going to manage to find a fairly good place to live together, but I refused to worry about it. Something would present itself at the right time.

To start with, Kevin would stay with me in the nurses' home until we could find a more suitable place. The main thing was to just go about my daily routine, happily and healthily.

I was over the moon when my husband arrived after 4.5 months of being separated! The BEST was yet to come: our baby, in just over 2 months!! Just about a week after his arrival, one of our friends asked if we would be interested in checking out a 2-bedroom, ground floor "flat" (the term for an apartment in England). We took a look and decided that it was acceptable for our home. See how things tend to work out well without worrying? Everything and everyone is interconnected and is supposed to work well in harmony.

I resigned from my job at the eye ward in early February, 4 weeks prior to March 8, my EDL (expected date of labour).

To ensure a smooth and easy childbirth, it is highly recommended for women in late pregnancy to walk a lot. That's what Kevin and I did daily. It was winter in England, but the temperature was pretty mild, around 7 to 12 degrees Celsius. My recollection was during that time, we savoured our togetherness so much. We were in great harmony, anticipating the sweet fruit of our love for one another.

At 5:30 in the morning, on March the 8th, I was awakened by quite a strong contraction, followed by another and another, regularly, every few minutes. That was the sign of labour I had been waiting for.

We got ready to go to the hospital and, within half an hour, we were at the hospital.

I was very familiar with the routine procedures I was to have, so I was naturally feeling quite trusting as well as excited. Very soon, I would be able to see our baby.

Our first baby girl, Angellyn, (we call her Angie), was born at 13:20, on the exact date of my EDL. She came out quietly and peacefully, trying to observe her new surroundings. What an angelic face!! Both Kevin and I kept staring at her in wonderment. All my hard work during the last two hours of labor was forgotten in a flash. It was such a blissful experience, a moment that I could still capture vividly many, -many years later. How could I forget? All the wonderful moments should easily be treasured and recaptured from the core of our beings. This is the secret to being happy and positive at all times. On the other hand, any negative experience should just be acknowledged and the meanings searched, and then it should be thrown out and never brought to mind anymore. Give it a proper burial with a good ceremony.

I always go by this principle. Since I keep on disciplining myself to adopt this attitude, it gets easier as the years go by. It starts with understanding the concept, then just keeping on doing it. When I practice it multiple times, it eventually becomes my habit. Just like that!

A little setback from taking our bundle of joy home was that she had persistent jaundice. She needed 3 days of phototherapy to bring down the amount of bilirubin in her blood.

On day seven, we were given clearance to take her home. Oh, what joy we felt…

Back to U.K.

Parenthood was quite a harmonious and enjoyable task for both of us. Even weaning her from using diapers went without a hitch. We even managed to get her to sit down to do her daily bowel movement, on the pot, when she was just about 4 months old.

So, although she still wore diapers till 2 years old, she did not soil the diaper; she just wet it with urine. It helped with her skin, and the management of diaper changes too, especially since disposable diapers were not available at that time. We had to use cloth diapers and wash them in a small mechanical washing apparatus.

When Angie was 3 months old, I went back to work doing permanent night shifts from 9 p.m. till 7:30 a.m. She slept through the night by that time, which was easier for Kevin to manage. Unfortunately, Kevin could not do any legal paying job, as his application for a permanent resident was declined. He did some odd jobs helping our friends, such as doing some light renovations in their houses.

We decided to apply as permanent residents of Canada. After waiting for about 4 months, we were lucky to be accepted based on Canada's need for civil engineers at that time. We needed to enter Canada within two years of that acceptance.

Ever since I had given birth to Angie, every morning, I dreaded doing "number two" (bowel movement).

My family doctor sent me to a specialist, and it happened that I had anal fissures as a side effect of pushing the baby out. The remedy would be surgical repair under general anaesthesia.

In the meantime, I was advised to eat lots of fruits, such as oranges and prunes, to ensure daily soft stools. I could recall my dread each morning quite clearly. In the end, I requested to have surgical repair. By that time, we had already made arrangements to fly back to Indonesia.

The surgery to repair my anal fissures was done two days prior to our flight to Jakarta. It all went very well, and the three of us happily flew back to Indonesia.

Kevin and I tried to sell our newly built house in Bogor. The plan to enjoy the house that was supposed to be our first home, did not materialize. We both did not mind it too much, as living in Canada beckoned to us strongly. Kevin got a summer job in rural Ontario, Canada, when he was a second-year student of Leeds University, U.K., and he loved the country there and then.

We stayed in Bogor with my parents. They were very happy to accommodate the three of us. Angie was 15 months old at that time and was being the centre of attention from all of us. She is my parents' first grandchild. That made it all the more special for them to cater to all her wants.

Back to U.K.

Added to this was her angelic temperament. Such an idyllic time we all had! It's such a beautiful and blissful memory whenever I look back to that wonderful togetherness.

After staying about two months, we decided to get ready to start a new life in our chosen country of Canada. My parents' neighbor had a sister and brother-in-law who lived in Toronto.

They agreed to allow Kevin to stay in their apartment temporarily until he found a suitable place for the three of us. We booked our flight to London, England. The plan was for Kevin to fly solo from there to Toronto, Canada, while Angie and I would stay with a very dear friend of mine, Helen, who had a boy of 5 years old. Our plan went smoothly.

Chapter 7

Toronto, Here I Come

"The will to win, the desire to succeed, the urge to reach your full potential, these are the keys that will unlock the door to personal excellence."
Confucius

Angie was such a happy-go-lucky girl, that when her dad hugged and kissed her goodbye at London Heathrow Airport, she remained cheerful and chatty. She was 18 months old at that time.

After just one week of waiting, Kevin wrote that a place was ready for us for the following week.

I booked the flight to Toronto for both of us, to be together as a family again. During the 7-hour flight, Angie was quite restless! She was only quiet when I stood up cuddling her.

I was feeling quite tired by the end of the 7-hour flight, but I was very energized by the warm welcome extended to us by the immigration officer. I really could feel that Canada was going to be my "home sweet home."

On our first night in Toronto, I realized that Angie's face was quite flushed with fever, so I decided to give her some Tylenol syrup to bring her temperature down. She needed the dose every 4 hours throughout the night, which indicated that we should take her to see a medical doctor. We took her to the Hospital for Sick Children. The doctor told us that both her ears were infected and that they should respond well with antibiotic treatment. That was the reason for her being miserable all the time during the flight from London to Toronto. The moment we got off the plane, she was her usual active and pretty happy self again, although the fever was raging in her tiny body.

Within the same day of the antibiotic treatment, her temperature was down to normal, without the need for any more Tylenol syrup. That was a great relief to both Kevin and me.

Our first rental accommodation was only a very small bachelor unit with a kitchenette, which Kevin had booked for a month. Since we had no one to guide us on how to find a good rental apartment, Kevin just phoned someone with an Indonesian name. It just so happened that this man, Frans, was a very friendly and caring man, who invited us to his home and embraced us warmly. He even cosigned for our first rental apartment. He was a Godsend indeed.

Chapter 8

Back to Nursing Career

"Thoughts are mental energy; they are the currency that you have to attract what you desire. You must learn to stop spending that currency on thoughts you don't want."
Wayne Dyer

In my opinion, secretarial work in Toronto gave less pay and less satisfaction than the nursing profession. I was very happy knowing this fact, as my 5.5 years of training in England would be utilized as my career in Toronto.

I started going to a nursing agency to find some work. It was very easy for me to get work as a nurse. Mind you, the work was not as a registered nurse. I needed to take 2 whole days' exams to work as an RN. I was assigned to work as an auxiliary nurse/nurse aid in a nursing home.

At the same time, I was on the lookout to get some work that would be better than lifting many elderly people in nursing homes.

I saw an ad in the Toronto Star, for a medical clinic that was in need of a nurse to assist doctors. I jumped at the opportunity and called for an interview. After just about two weeks working in the nursing home, it was a big blessing that I was accepted to work in a medical clinic. The work hours were Monday to Friday, from 9 to 5. I felt privileged and grateful for my first full time job in Toronto. The working atmosphere was very pleasant, and the work was very easy.

Meanwhile, Kevin was also busy, applying for jobs as a civil engineer or estimator. It took him about three weeks before he landed one. Little Angie had to go to a baby-sitter during the day when both of us worked. Luckily, we found a good and reliable one immediately.

As soon as we settled in our jobs, I started gathering data as to what the procedures were to sit for the exams to get my RN certificate. Within four months of my arrival in Toronto, I got my RN certificate. I then went back to the nursing agency and requested a placement as an RN.

They sent me to various hospitals in downtown Toronto, and upon the realization that I would earn about double my salary than I would at the clinic, with a heavy heart, I resigned from my first full time job in Toronto.(after only three months there).

After about ten months in Toronto, we felt ready to own our first house. Kevin and I would drive around to see what house would take our fancy. We located one very fast.

Kevin called the real estate agent's number to see the house. We both liked it and were asked to go to his real estate office to make an offer. We signed the dotted line, and the offer was accepted.

That was the time of high interest rates, 15% seller's financing for 3-year term. Looking back, after I became a real estate agent myself, I realized how easy we were in making our decisions. So many people think that they have to have a perfect house first time around. We were both very practical and aware that there was no such thing as a perfect house. We could always upgrade whenever we felt ready to spend more money for our "castle."

Owning your house is always better than renting. Hence, we were out of the rental situation in one year, and feeling very happy about this.

A couple of months into our home ownership, we had exciting news! Our property that Kevin had built in Bogor, Indonesia, was SOLD, just in time for us to reduce the amount of our mortgage.

After this payment, we felt that we could move to a bigger house.

As destiny might have dictated, a realtor dropped her business card in our mailbox after we had been in our first house for one year. I called her and asked her to come to see our house and she came by that evening. If we could break even, after the legal and realtor's costs, we would be happy to sell. She agreed to list it for sale.

We only had 2 showings of the house during the five days that the house was on the market. One made an offer to buy. We signed the Agreement of Purchase and Sale, at 10 p.m.

After the signing of the contract, and with both realtors gone, we had a pang of regret and worry due to the uncertainties of what kind of house we would find next. The following day, I called 2 lawyers and asked if we could get out of the deal that we, had just signed the night before. Both lawyers said the same thing, that it would be in our best interest to proceed with the transaction. So, we gritted our teeth and started the process to look for another house. Within 10 days, we found our 2nd house. The closing date was 5 months away.

My subsequent goal was to be able to drive around instead of having to rely on public transport. I did learn to drive once (comprised of 6 one-hour lessons), in the U.K., using a manual car. I did not like it, and since the public transportation was very convenient, I just abandoned the idea of being able to drive a car in London.

Now, in Toronto, the public transportation was not as good as it was in the U.K.; plus, the weather was much colder, and importantly, another crucial factor: Kevin's impatience when we shopped!!

I strongly felt that being able to drive was a priority that I must master. I started the process to obtain my driver's license; I took 12 1-hour driving lessons. On my tenth lesson, my driving instructor said that I should just go for a driving test. She booked it at the airport location. All these 10 hours, I never asked Kevin to take me on the road for my practice. On the day prior to my driving test, I thought I should practice with Kevin next to me, in a parking lot. It was not a good idea at all. Only patient and besotted husbands might try. I swore that I would never practice driving with Kevin again: never, never, never, ever!!!

I did my driving test at the airport location. It was very confusing as the road was only used for the road test, and not for the public at large. Needless to say, I failed.

My driving instructor was sympathetic and booked another test for me in Aurora, with a real public road, north of Toronto, about 60 km out of the busy city. The test was just three weeks away.

I showed Kevin the paper that was given to me, with all the points of the mistakes I had made.

He was quite calm while accepting the fact that I had failed the road test. I purposely omitted the fact that another test was booked for me to redo it in three weeks' time, for fear of his strong opposition.

On the second driving test, I prayed with all my heart that God would guide me in this task , even to completely take over during the half hour test. I felt so NOT ready for the road test, not having had any practice in between the driving lessons, but I was very strong in my belief that God would miraculously hover above me to make me appear confident and competent behind the wheel…Thoughts and prayers, especially, are mental energy. They are the currency that you have in order to attract what you desire. The power of attraction was about to unfold before my very eyes.

In my mind, having a driver's license would enable me to practise by myself without having to have Kevin sneer at me during the drive.

It was so surreal that I was indeed feeling very calm and composed during the road test.

After the test, the kind examiner congratulated me on passing!! I PASSED the road test!! Yippee!

That was for sure a miracle. I was beside myself with the magnitude and gratitude of passing.

Later that evening, I felt that I needed to test Kevin's reaction if I were to tell him that I did my 2nd attempt at the road test...and failed again. I showed him the previous paper, where I had failed.

I am happy to say that he passed my test. He was not violently angry, but quietly read the paper that I gave him. Then he mentioned that the paper stated the same mistakes I had made during my first road test, and he then glanced at the date. He realized that he had been given the same paper from the three weeks prior, and I could not stand the suspense anymore; I quickly gave him my passing paper, with roaring, hearty laughter. Alleluia, God answered and granted my sincere prayer! I felt so blessed and privileged to have passed the road test the 2nd time around.

My next goal was to be able to drive on the highway, after I gained confidence driving locally.

To be able to master my driving, I had to drive as often as possible. That was quite enjoyable to do, such as driving to the grocery store and other shops, and picking up Angie from school. One day, a thought came to mind that if I were to be a visiting nurse, then I would have more time driving on the road.

Without any delay, I acted on that thought by applying to St. Elizabeth Visiting Nurse. They accepted my application after a lengthy verbal interview of over one hour. It was a pleasant interaction though. They had to make sure that I was level-headed and able to function without any supervision, and ready to deal with all sorts of challenges in people's homes. I was very pleased having this opportunity to do lots of driving, as well as the prospect of being totally independent in my daily work. So, this was another win-win choice!

I started as visiting nurse sometime in March, and by October, with the thought of winter driving, my common sense nudged me that I should apply to work in a hospital, on permanent night shifts.

Whenever I have an inkling to do something, I act on it as soon as my time permits. I immediately wrote to Mount Sinai Hospital for a permanent night shift at NICU (Neonatal Intensive Care Unit), for Monday, Tuesday, and Wednesday nights, from 7:30 p.m. to 7:30 am.

I had worked there quite a few times through a nursing agency. The staff seemed to like me, and the feeling was mutual, as often is the case.

Very soon, I had an acceptance letter from Mount Sinai Hospital. I gave 1 month's notice to St. Elizabeth Visiting Nurse. By this time, I had mastered the local driving competently. The highway driving was not mastered yet. It was still in its infancy. Since the need was not quite there yet, I just left it on the back burner.

Kevin did not want me to drive home after my night shifts. He insisted on driving me to the subway station in the evening, and I would come home by subway, followed by bus, to get home after my night shifts.

Life fell into a good routine for a couple of years, until my second child was born. Angie was 6 years old when Annmarie came into our world. We purposely spaced the 2 children that way, so that we could concentrate our attention on one at a time. Angie would be in school all day while Annmarie needed lots of care as a newborn baby.

At that time, the maternity benefit was only given for twelve weeks after childbirth. I started back to work in NICU of Mount Sinai Hospital, only from 7:30 p.m. till 11:30 p.m., for 4 to 5 evenings per week. On Saturdays and Sundays, I was often called for a 12-hour-shift, from 7:30 a.m. to 7:30 p.m.

Juggling between career and raising children was quite interesting for me—never any dull moments!

My priority had always been the health of the 2 girls. Whenever one or both of them were unwell, I would just call in sick to enable me to give proper care to them. With great pride, I recollected that although both of them had some bouts of asthma when they were very young (-from age of 3 to 8-), they both had never been hospitalized. I was very vigilant with their care. I guess, I was used to caring for sick babies during the acute stage. I could intervene, during the night or day, to give more doses of inhalers to open up the air passages, before they collapsed and needed an oxygen tent. This treatment could only be given in the hospital. Happily, I have managed their condition very well, so that there was never any need for either one of them to be hospitalized.

In school, the little children were pushed to play outside. I believe that when one is unwell, one has to be kept warm indoors, especially in the case of small children. Each time Angie or Annmarie had a cold, I would make sure that I was home to give them proper care at home. It really paid dividends!

Both Angie and Annmarie did splendidly well in school; they ranked number one at the end of each school year till grade 12. We were quite happy in our day-to-day lives. Kevin was the disciplinarian, and I acted as the soft cushion for them to take refuge in. The first two decades of our marriage were very harmonious. Kevin and I had totally different careers; he was the president at his welding company, and I was an NICU nurse. The second two decades had a very different flavor indeed. Some of the difficult challenges will be narrated and shared with you here, as a tool for some of you when your marriage changed drastically from simple to complex.

Kevin's career was advancing nicely. He was given a brand new company car by his second employer. He stayed there for almost five years. All financial matters in our household were managed by him.

I just worked, and all my paychecks went directly into our joint bank account. He was in charge of paying all the bills from our joint banking account. We managed to accumulate enough of a down payment for our first income property, which was just next door to our house.

Many people are scared to manage tenants, just because they have heard how tenants can make your life very miserable. This is very unfortunate indeed. If you are too busy/too scared to manage your tenants, you can always find someone to do this. You just have to do what the bible says: "Seek, then ye shall find." Later, I will tell you more about how my tenants were managed (by me) from Toronto, after I purchased a property in Clearwater, Florida, and another one in Vancouver.

The main thing that you have to understand is the simple concept of how investment in properties is the easiest way to accumulate wealth. So many books and seminars are available to further educate you. I am not going to elaborate my understanding about this concept; I'm just going to share with you, that I feel so blessed to be able to really embody the simple understanding, and am able to run with it.

Kevin left his second employment, together with three of his colleagues, to open a new welding company that lasted for 14 years. Towards the end of the partnership, Kevin was preoccupied with buying and selling shares online. His preoccupation with the stock market soon became an addiction that consumed his waking hours. Initially, I was highly anxious, to the extent of helplessness. Sharing my anxiety with his mother, aunt, and sisters did not help the matter at all.

What helped a great deal was my solid faith. I totally surrendered to my ever-loving Father, and very soon was given assurances that all would be well and I would be blessed with abundance!!

Chapter 9

Realtor as My Third Career

"When written in Chinese, the word, 'crisis,' is composed of two characters; one represents danger, and the other represents opportunity." John F. Kennedy

Kevin and I managed to also get Annmarie to sit on her potty to have her bowel movement, as soon as she was able to sit straight, at about 4 months old. It was easier with her. In a department store called K-Mart, we bought a little chair for babies, with a pot in the middle and a little plastic table in front.

This chair looked like a miniature commode (what we used for an adult patient who couldn't walk well due to a stroke, usually). Our kids had the habit of having their bowel movement first thing in the morning.

It was easy for me to feed her in the morning, and then sit her on that miniature commode, with some rattles to keep her occupied while I tidied the crib and the room.

The disposable diapers were just wet from 4 months on. This was a WIN-WIN situation for both my baby and me: the child's skin was protected and I, as her main caregiver, did not have to endure the unpleasant job cleaning the messy, smelly chore. Furthermore, the training was so seamless and effortless.

When Annmarie was 6 years old, Kevin and I started to feel that we should move to a bigger house, as we felt we would be able to afford a higher monthly payment by this time. I started to check out how I could be a licensed realtor, to enable me to get paid when I sold and bought my own properties.

Within six months, I passed all the requirements to start my third career, which was originally supposed to be just my sideline job.

My main job was that of being an RN (registered nurse) at Mount Sinai Hospital, the place where I have spent half of my waking hours—my second home, I could say. I was quite happy and contented doing my job, first by physically caring for the tiny premature babies; and second, by being able to answer the questions for the parents of the babies, and guiding them to handle their precious tiny babies.

It was very satisfying to be a part of life's miracles that would unfold before my very eyes. The babies that were born after only 24 weeks' gestation, who would have died had it been many years ago, were now able to survive satisfactorily.

I really thought it was my calling to do the job until retirement; during weekdays, I would do night shifts, and on weekends, I would do day shifts. My working hours were full-time or a little bit more than full-time hours, without full commitment on my part. My girls were definitely my priority. I could take off sick without pay whenever I needed to be home to tend to my precious girls. Obviously, I was not given any health or dental benefits at all, and Kevin had no benefits either, since he had opened his own company just a few months after Annmarie was born. Thank God, we were all blessed with good health.

When Angie was 10 years old (Annmarie was 4), our next door neighbor asked if we were interested in buying their house. We jumped at the opportunity, thinking that one of our daughters might want to live next door to us. After a week or so of it being empty, I put an ad in the newspaper to get a tenant, which would help with our monthly mortgage payment. It was quite easy to find a tenant— within just a week!

After I had my realtor's license, just prior to buying our next house, I often wondered how to get clients to buy or sell properties. Lo and behold, my former classmate, from the real estate course, asked me to find a tenant for her condo apartment, as she must have trusted me more than she trusted herself. I took the job happily, and I advertised in a medical residence, through my colleague at Mount Sinai Hospital, who lived there.

One of the doctors who lived there asked me to show the 3-bedroom unit that was advertised. I met with him and his wife in the unit, and I asked them if they had ever thought about buying instead of renting.

They seemed to agree that buying would have made more sense, since they were quite qualified to buy their first house, if I was willing to guide them. "With great pleasure," I answered, with a beaming face.

See...since I was willing to do the work, it opened another door that was far more lucrative than anything I had ever anticipated—just baby steps, one in front of the other. Before I knew it, my journey turned out to be colorful, exceeding my expectations. I experienced it time and time again.

In 1994, after one year of being a realtor, the government gave incentive to homebuyers that they could use $40,000.00 of their RRSPs as a down payment for a house, without having to pay the penalty of using the RRSP money.

The repayment of the RRSP was also quite attractive, (i.e., within fifteen years). We jumped at this opportunity, and I paid commission to myself on the purchase of the house that we still live in currently.

By agreeing to do rentals to help someone out, I ended up getting tenants for that 3-bedroom unit belonging to my former real estate classmate, and a buyer, too! Three of my colleagues at Mount Sinai Hospital also bought properties through my help. It was just through word of mouth only.

Two years went by without any sign of substantial revenue for my real estate work. Then came a recession, and the NUA (nursing unit administrator) had to cut down the nursing staff to bare minimum.

Many of us permanent part-timers lost our regular schedules, from at least 3 of 12-hour shifts, to none at all. All nurses affected, went to her office, with so much anxiety. I was the only one, who (after seeing and hearing that the outcome of appealing to the NUA was futile) decided that worrying and complaining would get me nowhere. Instead, I felt that this supposed setback would actually help me to spend more time in trying to make a living through being a good realtor, with creative financing as my niche/specialty. I remember very, very vividly that I verbalized my high hope to a few nurses at that time. I said: "One day, I will thank this NUA for removing my three 12-hour shifts from my schedule!" I really felt very hopeful of doing more sales in real estate transactions, if only I could give more time and effort in this field. That was my gut feeling, and after a few incidences that supported this inkling, I concluded that very likely I would experience my positive instincts becoming a reality.

The quiet time in NICU lasted just for a couple of months. That was enough time for me to jump start my new career in the real estate world. I spent much of my time on the phone, calling friends and people I knew, to introduce my new endeavour; and whenever I shopped, I would also give out my business cards.

All those activities gave me very good results. I started feeling more and more confident in my dealings with my buyer-clients, who very often became my seller-clients in a few years' time.

When the NICU required me to work more hours, I limited my hours to usually just two 12-hour-shifts.

I started loving my real estate work better than my nursing job. I specialized in the financing aspect of difficult deals, and at that time, I registered myself as a mortgage agent, only for one year. I would preapprove all my would- be buyers, and I ensured, that they would be able to get the key to the property they chose. When there were some glitches a week or two prior to closing, such as their car loan having to be paid off, I had some private lenders I could go to, so that my clients were protected. One time, I had a referral client who was preapproved by his realtor, and after five weeks of searching for a property, he found the one he loved. He was very excited and put an offer on that property, but three days later was told that his mortgage application was denied. Understandably, he was so incensed about this. One of his friends (my former client) advised him to quickly ask for my help to get that house through my service. I preapproved him properly, and concluded that I would be able to get him the mortgage he needed.

I then asked him to cancel his offer and, in turn, put my name, in trust, as the buyer for the same property that he had to cancel due to the fact that he was denied a mortgage. He was so thrilled with the whole amazing experience that he became very active, ready, and willing to promote me whenever anyone was in the market to buy or sell properties. I have a few of these people in my marketplace, thankfully. These people could see and feel that they were being the beneficiaries of my knowledge, connection, and compassion, and could benefit greatly from the wealth of the expert negotiator that I was (and still am, of course). I am well connected with a variety of lenders and other people to make their big move a pleasant experience.

All the financing knowledge I had was precipitated by my second purchase of my house. At that time, Angie was only three years old, and my realtor could not/did not want to spend the time to help me get a mortgage. I was feeling anxious about how I could get a commitment from a lender as soon as possible, despite the fact that the closing date was five months away. I had to spend a long time on the phone talking to several mortgage brokers, while Angie must have been feeling dejected. At that time, I made a resolution, and I promised myself that if I were ever to be a realtor, I would be different.

I would be more accessible to my clients after they signed on the dotted line. That good intention must have been a factor in my being blessed with a career that I enjoyed, which I am still enjoying immensely until now. The drawback to being a realtor is that even when working hard to show properties, and having an open house etc., there is no guarantee of being compensated. The money will only come if and when the deal closes. Working as a nurse was pretty rewarding and secure, and yet I felt that the calling to substitute it with being a real estate broker was quite strong and persistent. I wondered why. Well, I was following my passion, and from day-to-day, I would surrender myself to let God guide my destiny.

May I always be the light, or reflect the light, to make a difference in a good way, no matter big or small, to the people around me. In times of uncertainty or even calamity, I always remind myself that the BEST is yet to come. Many times over, I could see that the opportunities were almost always precipitated by some calamities. Just brace yourself in that ride; put one baby step in front of the other, steadily.

All will be well, or even much better, beyond your wildest expectation.

After approximately four years juggling my double tasks as an RN and a realtor, I had to quit my RN career as it took a toll on my health when I had to stay up all day after my 12-hour-night shift.

Usually, it fell on the closing date (or a few days prior) of my client's purchase. Remember, my specialty is financing; many things have to be ironed out to package the deal satisfactorily till the exciting conclusion of getting the key to the new house.

Prior to my resignation from Mount Sinai Hospital, around 1 a.m., when I just got back from my offer presentation, I was given a positive sign to move forward. This time, the sign was in the form of an advertisement with several testimonies, which gave me the good feeling that I should be able to exceed my pay as an RN, plus have a lot more job satisfaction. My mind was made up, and it was a great feeling of relief to have arrived at this decision. I had been praying for a while that this would be a good way to take.

I always feel grateful that I was blessed with the gift of faith. Without this feeling, I have been witnessing firsthand how people grapple with so many uncertainties as to how to solve certain complicated issues.

The simple issues could even become complicated if you tackle them incorrectly.

At the following shift, after that early morning revelation, I submitted my resignation from Mount Sinai Hospital. Ever since that time, I never regretted my decision one little bit. My career as a busy practicing realtor just took off, with so much satisfaction to be helping people with the largest investment of their lives. The fact that I focus mostly on the needs of my clients, the money comes as the byproduct of my wholehearted service. It gives me such a good feeling to be the instrument of my clients' needs in their real estate transactions.

The time that my real estate career flourished coincided with Kevin's decline in his company's success. He started spending so much time trying to make his living from trading in the stock market.

This seemed to stem from his dissatisfaction with his partners in his welding company. The last twelve months in his company was awfully difficult to make ends meet. It was sad to witness the closing down of his company after about 14 years of operation. Well, nothing and no one lasts forever after all. Life goes on...

As the stock market trading was very unreliable, Kevin decided to join me in being a realtor, and he did all the courses within six months. Initially, I was not concerned about us being in the same field and the same company, 24/7; but after multiple times with my clients praising me in front of him, I noticed that Kevin was jealous of me.

It sounds farfetched and paranoid, right? It really was unbelievable, but it was true—and it was nightmarish!!

Kevin was the president of his company for fourteen years, and suddenly, he had to witness that I was the one receiving praises, instead of him. This made him quite resentful towards me. Working together, 24/7, with Kevin was indeed very, -very challenging, and not good for our marriage. Luckily, my positive and hopeful character helped tremendously. If not by the grace of our good Lord and my faith in Him, our marriage would have been dissolved during the sixteen years that Kevin and I worked in the same field.

Three years down the road, while working in the same company with Kevin, I decided to open my very own company, in 2003, and this turned out to be a very good move for me. I managed to grow my self reliance a great deal. We did our deals separately, which lasted for three years. After that, Kevin decided to join my company, "as to save us money." Was it worth it??

Now, looking back, I realized that I was given a spiritual test, to strengthen my understanding and compassion in dealing with such a very sensitive issue. I am humbled to say that, after 16 years of working in the same field with my husband, "Yes! I needed to experience all the difficulties, and now, have passed the test."

In 2016, Kevin decided to relinquish his realtor's license.

I have passed the tricky trials with flying colors!!

Chapter 10

Living in the Flow of Now

"Once you no longer need the lessons in your life that unpleasant events offer you, you will no longer experience these events." Wayne Dyer

In my life journey, I have been adding some proactive effort to prevent some unpleasant events from reappearing. This world is a giant school of LIFE. I consciously aim to enjoy every breath I take, not by chance but by design.

In the previous chapter, I mentioned how tough it was to have a business partner, who was jealous of my results. It was really beyond me how this could be happening to me! Instead of feeling downtrodden, I just concentrated on my tasks at hand. Whenever I was extremely busy with my activities in helping a few clients with each of their pressing needs, I noticed that somehow my mind was not bothered at all with the difficulties facing my teammate's negative treatment of me. I was literally too busy to cater to anything else; I concentrated on my duty to do my best for my clients.

I had to focus on my tasks at hand rather than reacting to Kevin's negative onslaughts. What a tricky situation for me, *if* I allowed it to be. Instead, I purposely had some mercy on him. I just kept focusing on doing a good job for my clients, and I brought meals home after my work on the road, to be enjoyed together.

I would switch the focus to a lot of other things whenever faced with our differences which were plentiful. It became very clear to me that our thoughts were so different. Well, opposites attract!

It became a nonissue to me, fortunately for our marriage! The day Kevin decided not to carry on working as a realtor, after about 10 years in my company, I felt such a relief. I passed my 16 years of trials, working in the same field with my husband, who was often mean towards me. I frequently had to walk on eggshells, afraid of bruising his ego, whenever we were out working together as a husband and wife team.

I am now postulating my predicament, I see the harmony I so craved with my husband will materialize very soon. I'll savour it gratefully and appreciatively. Kevin and I are going to start collaborating consciously, and both of our daughters will be so impressed with this miracle, unfolding before their very eyes.

I have now arrived at my golden years fully prepared for "The BEST is yet to COME!"

My understanding of all the lessons in my trials and tribulations is now helping me to help others (who are in need of my help) in my life.

I would always be an encourager to anyone, to replace any negative traits, such as anger, jealousy, hatred, with all the positive traits such as love, compassion, joy and peace. You have to be the change you want to see, and hopefully my family and close friends will just automatically realize and adopt this attitude too.

If not, their mental health will surely be compromised, just as what happened to the two people mentioned in this book (Dee and Tom), later in this chapter, under "Mind Your Mind."

Early on in my real estate business, I decided to open my own personal banking account to prevent Kevin from using my money for his stock market trading. This was a huge preventative measure indeed, as two years later, he suffered from a big loss in his stock market trading.

I had been spared from my family's financial trouble through following my gut feeling. My guardian angel had urged me to take action, and since I was proactively in tune with my higher self, I took action accordingly.

OUR VERY FIRST PET: "Winnie"

One of my clients, Sarah, had a cute female puppy of Shih Tzu breed, named Winnie. Five months after she bought Winnie, she decided to take up a second job to enable her family of four (husband and 2 kids) to have some finer things in life to enjoy. This caused Winnie to be sort of neglected. Sarah offered me to adopt Winnie for free. I was not too sure about having a puppy to take care of. I asked Sarah if it would be possible for Winnie to be cared for part time at first, 3 times a week, from 8:30 a.m. till 6 p.m.

Winnie was only about 7 months old; Angie was 20 years old, and Annmarie was 14 years old. Having a dog, man's best friend, is really an excellent idea to build character and instill responsibility into the children, provided the parents involve them and follow through. Never enable them to slack off or let them get away with neglecting fundamental obligations, such as feeding and maintaining cleanliness of the pet.

Growing up, I had always had a dog, and I enjoyed them immensely.

Angie and Annmarie were so thrilled to have Winnie around to play with. The work that comes with it was allocated to them too. Angie was more consistent in the duty of taking Winnie for daily (sometimes even twice a day) walks. After about one month of having Winnie three times a week, I asked them if they were ready for full-time ownership. They both answered with a definite resounding YES. This was another example of a WIN-WIN scenario that I so convincingly adopted in my daily life: Sarah was so relieved that Winnie had found a good home! Angie, Annmarie, and even Kevin were over the moon to have Winnie—and last but not least, me! I was beyond thrilled and grateful with this priceless gift; Winnie was such a jolly, smart, loyal best friend to all four of us.

One time, when I left for 10 days for holidays in China (Kevin declined to go due to his special client's need at that time), I had a very, very special welcome back from Winnie. She was jumping around for about 20 minutes and was very full of obvious glee. She must have thought that she had lost me for good. I savoured the ecstatic welcome a great deal, and I still recall it clearly, even after more than a decade later. It was one of the exceptional memories that I treasure lovingly.

There were two other incidents that stood out in my mind. The first one was when she was being the target of blame by Annmarie. Winnie had contracted some fleas, which were banished very swiftly by proper medication from her veterinarian. At that time, Annmarie was just diagnosed that she had eczema. She had thought innocently that Winnie's fleas might have been responsible for the intense itch that she suffered on her lower legs. She looked at Winnie with stern eyes and anger, and told the poor dog off with a harsh and accusing voice. Winnie looked back at Annmarie and answered indignantly with a confused sound, as if to say, "Why are you mad at me? I only want the best for everyone, and you are my best friend."

It was quite a phenomenon, one of a kind, seeing her trying to appeal her confusion. Winnie was not barking but mumbling her sentences.

Upon hearing Winnie's protest, both Annmarie and I laughed heartily at how the look, attitude, and tone of voice could trigger Winnie to sound like a human answering the accusation.

The second incident was at the park. We bumped into another dog, a Chihuahua, who was barking furiously at Winnie. She was quite cool when facing that fussy dog, and kept walking with us. (Winnie did not have a leash, but the Chihuahua was on a leash.). After about 45 seconds, Winnie just bolted and turned around. We did not know what she was up to. We just followed Winnie's lead until we were behind the Chihuahua. The Chihuahua felt the presence of Winnie and started to bark furiously again. Winnie was taunting her fussy friend with a little smirk on her face. She looked up at us and nodded her head to leave the noisy Chihuahua, for she must have given the Chihuahua a piece of her mind. We were tickled pink with her smart acts. She had to find the noisy dog again, to give her a piece of her mind...So hilarious!

Unfortunately, Winnie only lived for 6.5 years. She died due to a condition called "pyometra", i.e., pus collection in her uterus.

The signs she displayed were that of excessive urination coupled with vomiting. Angie (who just came by for the weekend) and I took her to our veterinarian that Saturday morning, and Winnie was scheduled to have surgery on Monday morning. In the meantime, she was going to be put on an intravenous drip.

I had begged the veterinarian to allow me to take her under my care at home, as I had been used to managing the premature babies with intravenous infusions for about 15 years. In that veterinary hospital, Winnie would be caged with no one around in the night.

I was very against this idea, but my plea fell on deaf ears! Reluctantly, I let Winnie stay without further protest, despite my strong conviction to be her voice of reason. The following day, Sunday afternoon, I came by to see how she was doing. She wagged her tail in the cage but looked somewhat lethargic. I just stroked her head for a few minutes while talking to the attendant about her course of antibiotic treatment.

Winnie was scheduled to have an intramuscular antibiotic treatment that afternoon, which was very strange indeed. She had to be pricked for that. My argument to just give the antibiotic through the intravenous line went unheeded as she was just following the order, and she tried to dissuade me that it was the correct way for animals. It did not make any sense at all.

Again, I had to just grin and bear this nonsensical idea. Never in a million years would I know that it was my last moment to see Winnie alive...

On Monday morning at 8 a.m., on June 25th, 2007, she was found dead by her veterinarian, and I was immediately notified. Angie had gone back to Canton, Ohio, USA, where she was doing her residency as a family physician.

The three of us—Kevin, Annmarie, and I—quickly went to the veterinary hospital to retrieve Winnie's physical body. We were asked if we would like to watch the autopsy to confirm the cause of death.

Robotically we did, with so much anguished and grief. Her uterus was filled with pus and removed.

What a sad day it was for all four of us in the family. This disease happens frequently to female dogs without litters. We did try to get her to mate with another Shih Tzu, but nothing happened as obviously it was not during "heat," the fertile period for Winnie.

OUR 2nd PET: "Lucky"

The three of us really missed Winnie so much that we decided to look for another puppy.

As luck would have it, we managed to find another Shih Tzu of 6 weeks old. We were very thrilled, and without any reservation, bought and brought that tiny puppy home.

This time, we had a male puppy. We named him "Lucky." Having a dog in our daily lives definitely added a spark in our day-to-day routine.

CAREER + FAMILY LIFE

I obtained my license as a realtor, in January 1993, and joined Canada Trust Realty for approximately one year. Being very new in this business, the company took 50% of my commission from each and every one of my transactions. After not even one year with this company, Canada Trust Realty closed down, and all the realtors were offered to join Coldwell Banker, with the same manager and office. I had a talk with the manager, who interviewed me prior to my joining the company. I requested a higher percentage for my part, as I did everything, including offer preparation. Most of the time, I worked from the comfort of my home. To my logic, he would grant my request, as he must have known that he hardly saw me in the office. Unexpectedly, he declined. His words were not very encouraging, or should I say, they were very dismissive.

Instead of feeling down, I did my routine conviction: the negative treatment had to be the catalyst for an improvement. Basically, I have a strategy to not waste any pain. The pain should produce gain! I saw this as an opportunity to expand my horizon.

I went to interview with two other broker owners to explore my options, and I was happy to pick Century 21 Eldorado as my next brokerage. It was indeed the right fit for me, with 75% commission given to me from each transaction. My first transaction with this Century 21 office was with someone who collected air miles. Century 21 was his target realtor, as we were able to reward clients with some air miles on the closing date. The moment he met me at one of my open houses, he was very happy to appoint me to be his realtor, to assist him with his move from his condominium apartment to a house.

I was the realtor for both his sale and purchase, which I would have missed had I stayed put at the old company with the new name (from Canada Trust Realty to Coldwell

Banker). I took the dismissal of my request with a positive attitude, followed by positive actions. It has worked time and time again for me when something was not flowing nicely; I take it as a sign for me to get out of the situation and find something else.

Now let me share the dynamic of our family during the college and high school years of our two daughters.

Those years seemed to be flying by so fast, as they were very busy almost all the time. Outside the study time, both girls did help out, either by answering telephone calls, faxing, or doing accounting for us.

Most of the time, I would bring ready-made foods for us all to enjoy. When I did try to cook, the phone calls from prospects and clients often ruined the process, such as having overcooked or burned foods.

The advantage of just buying the lunch/dinner on a regular basis, was that the owners of the restaurants/fast food' places got to know me well. They in turn became my clients.

Angie and Annmarie were both enrolled in piano lessons as their extra-curricular activities. Every evening I was home, Angie frequently asked me to play table tennis/ping pong. I enjoyed these games immensely, as it was a good physical exercise, and a good occasion to nurture Angie during her growing up years. I often recall those days longingly. Annmarie did not like to play ping pong. Instead, she would spend her spare time drawing beautiful portraits.

Angie's classmate asked her if she would be willing to do part-time secretarial work in a doctor's office that was owned by her dad, who was the only medical doctor in that practice. Angie was 16 years old at that time. She was quite thrilled about this and took the offer happily. Since she did not drive yet, Kevin or I had to chauffeur her to and from the doctor's office every Saturday.

We did it mainly to get her to gain experience in the work force, which could be an asset for a future job application. Annmarie took over that Saturday job when Angie left Toronto to do her medical degree in Saba Island.

I had no qualms in letting Angie do her post graduate study so far away, as she was level headed and goal oriented. Her choice was either pharmacy or medicine. She settled on medicine after we had a visit from Michael and Maria. Michael was Kevin's business associate who had taught him how to do online trading in the stock market. Maria (Michael's wife) was very friendly, and they both often included Kevin and me in their annual Christmas party at their beautiful house.

They encouraged Angie to do medicine, and this settled her choice nicely.

After 20 months of theory in Saba Island, she had to do the practical aspect of the curriculum, in USA. Her first placement was in Rochester, then Toronto, followed by New York City.

My eldest brother, sister-in-law, and their only son came along with us to attend Angie's graduation as a medical doctor, in Massachusetts. On the way back home to Toronto, we stopped in Maine to visit our former neighbor, as well as our schoolmate that both my eldest brother and I had not seen for decades.

That was a happy reunion indeed, and we all enjoyed the sweet lobsters that Maine is famous for.

Angie chose to do family doctor residency in Canton, Ohio, where she met and married Norman.

Meanwhile, Annmarie followed in my footsteps in choosing registered nursing as her career.

Kevin and I happily let Annmarie stay with us as long as she wanted. She only moved out to Vancouver due to her new job there and following her fiancée, who had moved there to be near his mother.

I managed to get Annmarie to invest in two properties during her stay with us. All management of the tenants were left to me. She was given a good return for the money she invested as down payment.

Not long after she moved to Vancouver, I returned all her down-payment money to free her to invest there. (more about this in the last chapter).

THE WONDER OF "ZHENG GU SHUI"

One day, suddenly, I had a swollen and painful right bunion. Luckily, it was summertime. I had to wear sandals, even to work in the hospital. I had good results using "Zheng Gu Shui" lotion after falling down while carrying Angie down the steps, hurting my ankle badly.

I missed one step of the stairs while carrying Angie from the car into the basement. As she was asleep, I picked her up gently. She was two years old and four months on that fateful afternoon. When I missed the last step of the stairs, I fell down on the ceramic floor with Angie, and she ended up on top of my ankle.

Oh boy, oh boy! The pain was very excruciating, indeed. Angie jolted up and watched me crawl in agony, and said:

"Nine one one, my mom needs ambulance, quick." Although in great pain, I was amused by her spontaneous comment. I asked her to go upstairs and get her dad to come to me urgently.

I had to crawl to the bed in the basement. When Kevin popped his head downstairs, I asked for an ice compress and two Tylenol tablets. Half an hour later, I asked for the Chinese lotion, Zheng Gu Shui, and applied the swabs soaked in that lotion for one hour.

Since that evening was my night on duty, I went to NICU Mount Sinai Hospital to take the report from the day staff, and excused myself to the emergency department to have an x-ray done and be assessed by a doctor. The doctor said that I had a hairline fracture and recommended a plaster cast to rest the ankle. I refused the immobilization by plaster cast, and I said that I would just tensor bandage it, plus apply the Chinese lotion.

He did not like my response, and said: "You nurses are impossible."

I just smiled and replied respectfully that I had a bad experience a few years back, and that during my plaster cast experience, for three weeks, from waist to ankle, the itch under the cast was too terrible to bear.

He advised me to go home, and I was given a pair of wooden crutches to use so that I would not have to put weight onto the Injured ankle.

I went back to NICU and waited for the ward clerk to find a replacement nurse, so that I could go home.

Unfortunately, no one was available, and I couldn't just walk away like that. My conscience would not allow me to do that. I ended up staying all night to complete my night shift. Some nurses helped me out, so I did not have to walk too much. I had two babies on ventilators, and the suctioning, plus the oral tube feedings, could be done while sitting in high chair.

I took 10 days off work to nurse my ankle. That Zheng Gu Shui lotion was very effective for me. It killed the pain and restored the blood circulation within a week. The swelling that reached to just under my knee initially, subsided gradually as the days went by. I put my right ankle up on a chair during the day, and elevated it on a pillow in bed during my sleep at night.

With very good results from the Zheng Gu Shui lotion for my ankle's hairline fracture, I also tried to treat the bunion with the same remedy. I compressed my right bunion with that lotion for one hour, followed by a few minutes of lotion application 3 to 4 times a day. After about ten days of self medicating using that Chinese lotion, to my great delight, my bunion was totally healed, without the need for surgery at all.

MIND + BODY CONNECTION

As I had more and more clients to take care of, I must have neglected myself quite a bit. There was no time to decompress at the end of each day. Gradually, with the stress piling up, I suffered from frozen left shoulder. I tried Zheng Gu Shui and acupuncture treatments about six times without any improvement at all. It was not incapacitating, but it was uncomfortable. I was stuck with the annoying discomfort for almost two years. One evening, I watched *Larry King Live*, and I felt an immediate connection with the topic about mind and body connection. Dr. John Sarno was being interviewed and was discussing his book, *Healing Your Back Pain*.

I felt that my frozen shoulder could be healed 100% if I were to understand and follow the instructions as precisely as I possibly could. There was a testimony from someone who experienced chronic lower leg pain, to the extent that he needed to use a wheelchair for weeks prior to applying Dr. Sarno's mind-body understanding.

Within a few days of changing his mindset, and with some physical exercises, he was able to heal his lower leg pain and was able to walk normally without any difficulty. How powerful one's mind can be! I felt exhilarated upon hearing this testimony; I promised myself to read the book thoroughly, and I applied my comprehension immediately. My first priority was to phone the bookstore to ask them to reserve a copy of Dr. Sarno's book for me to pick up. It was not as easy as I expected.

So many people were ahead of me. All copies in the stores were sold. I had to place an order through one of the bookstores and pick it up two days later.

The moment I received the book, I was fully convinced that I also would be able to heal my frozen shoulder. True to form, my frozen shoulder just went away within three days of reading and applying my understanding, plus with some simple exercises. It was yet another one of my miraculous experiences!! I recognized it gracefully and gratefully. When you do this each time you feel that you are helped by an unseen power greater than yourself, your life will be surrounded by more and more postulates like this. (Note: to postulate, means to manifest something in the physical world, by thinking it/saying it/writing it down). Another postulate of mine, was mentioned in the previous chapter, when I verbalized to my colleague at NICU, that I would thank the NUA for removing my scheduled working hours, to succeed in my entrepreneurial effort to be financially free, through helping other people in their real estate needs.

THE LAW OF THE UNIVERSE

The Universe always give you feedback on what you are doing. You have to be observant to participate fully in your life. I have a very dear realtor friend who was mean to his wife right in front of my very eyes. They sent their son to study abroad, which had been mainly decided between the wife and the son, as his self-employed business was not doing that well prior to their son's departure. His wife had been a successful dentist. A year later, he was blessed with a very good return on his business effort. His wife good naturedly asked him to start sending his money to their son. Unfortunately, for him, he was very mean when he answered: "You single-handedly sent him abroad without consulting me. Now you must follow through without involving me. It is totally on you!"

I was totally dumbfounded hearing his callous comments, and I told both of them that he had jinxed his good business by having that kind of attitude. He did not seem to care. I promised myself to follow the situation closely. We were in the same office at that time. For sure, I would easily find out, as all the new deals would be posted on the board. The law of the Universe cannot be challenged—it happened! All of his effort from that fateful incident did not bring any result at all. Hopefully, he learns his lesson fast, so that he becomes a nicer human being and transcends to a better place. Otherwise, he will go down further and further, as it is impossible for anyone to remain at the same place. Either you are growing, or you are dying, never status quo!

THE POWER OF INTENTION

It played out very early in my career as a realtor. I met a couple through an advertisement I had placed in a local newspaper. The couple were in their late thirties. They listed their basement to be rented out, and I managed to find them a good tenant.

After the transaction was completed, they told me that they had large debt on their credit cards, approximately $30,000 in total between the two of them. Since financing had been my niche from day one of my real estate career, I was able to arrange a low cost second mortgage pretty easily. Their house was co-owned by the husband's mother, who lived in Boston. They assured me that it would be no problem whatsoever to get her to sign the second mortgage paper. I made a big blunder, and the money was given to them without waiting for the mother's signature. It was a humongous indiscretion on my part, indeed! On the other hand, due to this very indiscretion, I could witness the power of intention at play.

A week after receiving the money, the couple told me that the mother refused to sign. I felt sick to my stomach and helpless, being under the mercy of this couple. I just hoped for the best, thinking that they would retain my services to list their house for sale down the road. The fact that they had to use my company when selling their property before paying off the loan, was fully explained to them and signed by that couple prior to their receiving the money.

Their monthly payments were irregular, to my great disappointment. The straw that broke the camel's back was when they sold the property using another realtor—and I found that out through my guardian angel's guidance. For an unknown reason, I was guided to show someone a house next door to the couple's house. After the showing, I just happened to see the couple, who were about to drive away from the house. I saw the SOLD sign on their lawn. Naturally, I approached them, surprised that they did not call me at all. Apologetically, the wife explained that her mother-in-law was the one in charge of the sale, and they were moving into her mother's house. I was just speechless, but I quickly asked for their new address so that I could mail a magnetic calendar, as it was early November and I had always sent my annual magnetic calendar to them around this time of the year.

That was so incredibly in the nick of time for me to be guided by the unforeseen force of goodness that I call my guardian angel. I felt it at that time; this couple were trying to run away from their responsibility to pay their loan. True enough, a few months down the road, they stopped their monthly payments. I went to talk to her mother, but to no avail. Just a block from her mother's house, I spotted a paralegal's office. I stopped by there and asked them to represent me in small claim's court. They asked me to furnish them with all the paper-works.

To make a long story short, we settled the amount that I was owed by that time, in small claim's court, to be paid monthly for the interest only; and the couple were allowed to pay the principal amount at any time, without penalty.

A few months went by smoothly until the payment was again stopped. This time, I decided to proceed without any help from any paralegals at all. We met in court again, and I won the case. The real irony was that the wife worked at a lawyer's office as a paralegal. I sent a letter to her employer, and to my sheer joy, I received all of my money back at last, after about five years of uncertainty.

Can you see how amazing the power of INTENTION was at play before my very eyes?? It was very humbling to me. When your INTENTION is good, you will always be recognized and rewarded. It was also a priceless lesson to always be mindful to not trust too much. All the required signatures have to be there before the money changes hands. Once bitten, twice shy! This enables you to progress nicely as you become more seasoned and experienced in both your professional and your personal life. You will keep on getting the same problem until you nail the solution for it.

Documentation is also very, very crucial; not only with clients but with blood relatives and best friends. No exceptions!! I learned this lesson very early in my career as a realtor. In the heat of the moment, if the plan is not in writing and without any details, conveniently you will be treated as if you were a leper.

It did not make me bitter at all, for that would be a waste of my pain. Always use your pain to your advantage. It's the same when you have labor pains. As a midwife, many years ago, I would always say to the woman in active labor: "Use your pain well, and push as hard as you can, so that you will be rewarded greatly; your baby is the end product of your pain!"

The same goes with everything else in life. Pay attention and participate well in all aspects of your life. Nothing should be accidental. Design it.

One day, when I had just started to build my real estate career, with financing as my niche/specialty, a very dear friend borrowed money in a time of need, and proper written promises were not in place at all, as I was very trusting. It caused us to be estranged for a few years, but we have now resumed our easy friendship with more understandings and renewed wisdom. That supposedly painful incident was very useful to me, in a way that, in my capacity as a Broker in a real estate transaction, I would put all details in writing, including the remedy for some possible circumstances. Again, I used the pain for some gain. We will never be afraid or anxious if we apply this knowledge.

Attending seminars regularly is a must for realtors, doctors, nurses, etc. Applied knowledge is POWER!!

These seminars cost quite a bit of money, but they are crucial to your professional development as well as your personal development. I attended many of them. A handful standout in my mind, and I would like to share these with you here.

LEASE TO OWN

The most beneficial seminar I took was "LEASE TO OWN," by Ross. It was the answer to one of my clients' needs. For about two years, this couple (who I will call Jane and John), in their early forties, was wondering how they would get out of debt of their second mortgage of $60,000, while they struggled to pay off their credit cards as well.

We met up at least twice to try to brainstorm how to get out of this large debt unscathed. After attending the 3 full days' seminar, Ross honestly stated that it was very rare that the attendees would practice the theories. Out of our class of 70, even if only one or two would apply the teachings, he would be thrilled. On the other hand, I was very excited postulating that this idea would fit handsomely with Jane's and John's situation. Without wasting too much time, I called John about my plan to "lease to own" their property for three to five years, to get them to be able to pay off their debts, in totality!

He agreed wholeheartedly and asked me to start advertising right away.

A couple of days later, I called John to ask him to open the door for a prospect. He said sure, and to just show the house. An hour later, dejectedly, he asked me to give Jane more time to accept their dire reality.

Apparently, she was depressed about their predicament. Two months later, John called and said that Jane had come to her senses, and that my suggestion was the only way they could be rid of their second mortgage.

It was not as smooth sailing as I would have liked it to be, however. The first couple were not able to carry on, and I had to ask them to leave. The house was then in need of a carpet change in the living room.

All was done by me without having to ask John and Jane for any money at all. I was their tenant, and I had to find someone that I could trust to "lease to own" from me.

A few days later, I found a mother and daughter who wanted to rent with the option to buy in three years' time.

I am happy to say that John and Jane were able to pay off the whole $60,000 second mortgage, with about $3,000 cash in their hands, just after 4 years. That was the beauty of owning a residential property. No matter how the economy is, people will always need a roof above their heads.

I also bought two properties after we sold our second house, which we had lived in for ten years. Kevin was not willing to put his share into another property as he was too much into the stock market. He said it was more liquid and easier, in his mind, to get a profit. He was quite misguided about this, as time would eventually show him...

The two properties I bought were advertised for lease to own, to practise what I had just learned in the seminar.

One property was still being rented to own by the same family, who never complained of anything else after a big basement leak that was funded through the house insurance. Most people would forfeit all the accumulated funds from the renters if they could not buy after a certain number of years. I do not plan to do that at all. I feel such great compassion to allow them to enjoy their "home sweet home." They are excellent in their monthly obligation to pay the rent, plus they have some savings that are being accumulated for their down payment.

Another house that was leased to own to a couple in their thirties, gave me quite a headache as their marriage ended in a divorce. The wife and the thirteen-year-old daughter wanted to stay on. Unfortunately, her payments were often late and not in full. After one year of giving her a chance, the time had come for me to inevitably evict this mother and daughter. The mother was not in court on the appointed date and, consequently, the judge ordered an eviction notice. Unfortunately, it had to be enforced by calling the sheriffs. They had to go into the house to ensure safety for Kevin and me. It was quite sad to see the state of the house that was left behind by the mother and daughter; it was very unkempt, and to make matters worse, the washing machine and dryer were stolen by them! I remained stoic, cool, and calm in that instance. I had a very strong conviction that the BEST was yet to come. I forbade Kevin to do any repairs or cleaning. Instead, I immediately placed an advertisement for a "rent to own" property.

Two prospects were very interested to take the unkempt house "as is." I settled on a couple that were in their early 40s, with a 12-year-old daughter. They were a handy couple and were used to the type of work that was needed around the house to make it shine. Three years down the road, they exercised their option to purchase, with some seller's financing for a few months, until they sold the house to one of their friends.

AFFIRMATION

Another seminar that stands out in my mind is Harv Eker's "NEVER TO WORK AGAIN," in Palm Desert, California. They asked all the attendees to repeat an affirmation: "I have massive passive income that I can spend this $... (to state the number individually, in accordance with your own reality) to my heart's desire." The number had to be an amount that you would think substantial, in your own opinion—not *too* outrageous, though. I participated in this exercise with gusto, joyfully and rigorously, and at the same time, I was also having so much fun anticipating the real outcome. This idea reminded me of the Christian teaching: "Ask and you shall receive." I am happy to say, that a few months later, my passive income grew to the amount that I had set during that fun seminar.

Also, NLP (neuro-linguistic programming) gave me some insights to participate in certain aspects of my life, with more understanding in the process. The breakthrough that was so amazing for me was that our subconscious mind is indeed more powerful than our conscious mind. You need to train your subconscious mind to focus on the outcome you want to see. A positive mind can be trained, indeed; and you can have real fun doing it.

Kevin and I worked as realtors for 16 long years: in the first 6 years he was with another company's brokerage, and ten years in my own company. My unwavering faith in practicing that love can conquer all, prevailed. The challenges were plentiful, I must say. Through them all, whenever I felt so overwhelmed, my nature was always to let go and let God. There was a two-year stretch of time where, I had episodes of night screams. I wrote a journal trying to understand what brought each episode into being. By being proactive, I did not let this unexplained phenomenon control/frighten me.

It appeared, that when Kevin showed strong disagreements directed at me, my subconscious mind protested, and the night screams would indicate that both of us needed to resolve the situation. I had 18 of them in that two-year span. Initially, the screams were piercing and loud. As I began to understand the triggers, they were much milder and much less scary. In the beginning of this strange phenomenon, I asked a Roman Catholic priest to bless our house…The light will always overcome the dark.

We also went to attend a weekend of "Retrouvaille" to get some perspective on how to not allow conflicts to consume us, and how to get reacquainted with one another again.

MIND YOUR MIND

In the interim, I witnessed 2 incidences that were quite an eye opener to take precaution or even to banish persistent negative thinking altogether. One was where a wife, Dee, was telling me how she hated her husband so much!! She went on and on about all her husband's faults that made me cringe. At that time, I felt strongly, she was going to have a mental breakdown or suffer insanity if she did not stop those negative thoughts. I told her to divert her thinking to something else that was pleasant to her, and even warned her, that she needed to be kind to herself, to prevent her from a mental breakdown.

When you have too much hate in your mind, it is like, you put poison into your own body, but expecting other people to die.

She was so consumed with the hatred towards her husband that she was so oblivious to what I said. Her husband had cheated on her, and her bitterness compounded the situation. She felt so repulsed by the cheating that she could never allow her husband to be intimate with her. A year later, I came to know that indeed she had become afflicted by mental illness, where for days on end she would not care for her personal hygiene or appearance. She had lost her sanity through her negative thinking that was not controlled or diverted in time. You should be very mindful about the facts that can and will harm your mental health. When I was in high school, I was drawn to be a psychiatrist. I knew back then however, that being a psychiatrist in the East, would not be a good choice for a career.

The demand was not there. People could connect to one another easily. In the Western world, the ease of connecting with other people is just not realistically available. Everyone seems busy with their own schedule.

That's why the demand for psychiatrists is much greater in the West, whereby everyone is too busy to make time for others.

The second incident was that a husband, Tom, lost his mental health due to his anger toward his wife for abandoning him for the sake of her reunion with some of her former classmates. He was so very angry about being left behind, that he suffered a stroke. After his stroke, he continued feeding his mind that his wife was responsible for his physical limitations, caused by the stroke. These negative thoughts led to his 2nd stroke.

He became blind after the second stroke, and he still raged on and on, feeling angry with his wife.

This anger caused him to lose his sanity, for he became a cantankerous old man and neglected his cleanliness, appearance, and refusal to clean himself after his normal bodily excretion. Luckily his wife was able to hire someone to help with his insane behavior. This went on for nine years before he died in misery. What a waste of two lives; people who used to love one another respectfully. So, you must always be mindful, NOT to grow your negative feelings, such as anger, jealousy, hatred. To always replace those negatives with all the positives you can think of, such as love, forgiveness, joy and peace.

His legacy was bad, too, for unfortunately, his mental breakdown lasted for unbelievably long, 9 years. What a waste of a smart mind he used to possess! Gone down the drain for lack of awareness!

MIDNIGHT MIRACLE

A few years ago, Kevin and I visited West Germany to see Mel following our trip to Eastern Europe.

Mel and I cycled to school together for six years, from grade 7 to 12. Over the years, although infrequently, we kept in touch through letters, telephone calls, emails, and WhatsApp. She paid me a visit in Toronto not long after her husband's passing, and we met again during our high school reunion. Mel and I maintained our friendship throughout the years.

Mel suggested to me that we should go to Frankfurt to see the Mercedes Museum there, and at the same time, we would be welcome to stay the night at Yuyu's (her sister) house. I declined this as I was already booked at a place close to Darmstadt.

We had a very relaxing evening at Yuyu's house. When we first arrived there, Yuyu showed Kevin and me that a bed was already prepared for us. I was touched by her kindness and hospitality.

I thought Kevin would take up this kind gesture, but I was mistaken. At 10:30 p.m., Kevin was determined to drive back to Darmstadt. I knew better than to argue, as once his mind was made up, he would not be swayed. What a scary driving experience it was! The road was dark, and there were so many roundabouts.

I just prayed throughout the journey, and miraculously could feel the spiritual being guiding Kevin during the drive. Once, we had to get off the highway to ensure that we were on the right path. We arrived at 1:30 a.m. and could not sleep till 3 a.m.

The following afternoon, we went to the place I had visited with Mel's brother many, many years ago: Heidelberg. As the weather was not that good, we just drove around the place.

Kevin had promised Mel that he would pick her up from Yuyu's place on our way back to Darmstadt. It was very unfortunate that Kevin kept on taking the wrong turn on the roundabouts, which were so frequent along the way. By 6:30 p.m., I felt that I should text message Mel about Kevin having to break his promise.

The next day, we had to go back to Toronto. I am postulating now that I will see Mel again, with some high school friends, in Singapore or Korea, or both, very soon. Well, we'll see!!

Chapter 11

Buying Properties in USA

"Don't give up control of your life to others. People respect you more when you operate from the position of strength and self-reliance." Wayne Dyer

Do not give up control, even to your flesh and blood, unless you're incapacitated mentally!

The moment our firstborn, Angie, and her husband, Norman, moved to Florida, I had an INTENTION to buy a property within a half hour drive from Angie's house, home away from our home in Toronto. It would serve two purposes:

1) Our stay in Florida could be as long as we wanted, without having to put up with any restrictions imposed, like you would if you were staying in someone else's home.

2) I would be showing by example how buying an investment property is a very good way to get your hard-earned money to work for you. Whenever you can buy a property, just buy. It will give you a handsome dividend down the road, guaranteed, as long as your investment results in a positive cash flow at the end of each month.

The above plan was carried out two years after Angie's and Norman's move to Florida. I booked a three week stay in Florida for the purpose of buying a suitable "home away from home."

It did not take us too long to find our best nest in Florida. We put an offer on a 1-bedroom townhouse to start with (did not go through), and then a 2-bedroom unit in a high-rise complex designated for over 55 years. This also did not go through. The third time was lucky, with a 2- bedroom unit townhome, which we still keep till today.

It was lightly used by the previous owner, who lived in New York City, and all the furniture, appliances, TVs, dinnerware, cookware, and linens were included in the price. I was somewhat apprehensive, though, about my obligation to pay for the monthly maintenance fees, property taxes, etc., if I were not able to rent it out for the months that we would be in Toronto. As soon as I realized the negative thoughts that I was projecting into the universe, I put these doubts out of my mind totally, and instead, replaced them with the thoughts of all the good things that would happen smoothly. Whatever you focus on, will come into being. Very often, people focus on what they don't like, instead of what they like. It's no wonder they keep on getting the very things they do not like.

An example is when I say: "Do not think of a pink elephant." What did you just think of? A pink elephant, right?

The subconscious mind needs to imagine all the desirable things you would be thrilled to have. Always anticipate abundance, for this is your birth right to experience. Believe it with all your heart, and you will see it. Happy are those who believe without having to see! It fits with the law of attraction too. You will attract the good things when you focus your mind on them with all your might, from the bottom of your heart.

True to my expectation, my "home sweet home" in Clearwater, Florida, attracted many people to rent. Six months down the road, we went back to Florida by car, taking our cute little Shih Tzu, Lucky, with us, as we planned to purchase a duplex with good long-term tenants in place. I envisioned it in my subconscious mind, and then got busy to locate such a property. I am happy to say that I found it after just five days of searching!

I put an offer in, and the offer got accepted. Two days down the road, Penny, the realtor, apologetically called; somehow there was a problem with the previous contract. It was supposed to have been cancelled and replaced by my contract. She was very distraught about this unexpected development.

I told Penny not to bother wasting her energy on getting upset over this peculiar and totally out of the ordinary transaction. I guessed she was embarrassed about this.

I said to her: "The BEST is yet to COME!" Then I asked her to show me the duplex that was on the same street, which had just come on the market. Yippee...I liked it even better. The tenants had been renting the duplex for many years, compared with the other one I had just lost, which had brand new tenants. Naturally, I put in an offer and I got it. Isn't it funny? When unexpected things come out of nowhere, do not despair, for they are going to be replaced by something better. I had these experiences many times with my transactions as a real estate broker. There are reasons for every season. By always accepting the inevitable, and facing the challenges bravely head on, you will do yourself a great favor. You better believe it; then you can start seeing the benefits. I was born with these basic understandings. Anyone can also copy this. You have to be willing to try this dogma first; understanding the concept and this good habit will then become your second nature.

On the way back to Toronto, we had to stay somewhere for one night as it was about a 23-hour drive. I booked a place that allowed a pet. On registering for the night stay, there was a big note displayed, saying that no dogs were allowed in the room. My heart fell; but at that time, I just decided not to say anything at all about the matter. This I felt would be the best action, as it would be more troublesome to have to look for another place. It was still bright outside at around 5 p.m. Since Lucky was only about 15 pounds, and a very quiet dog, it was not too hard to sneak him in and out in a bag. At about 2 a.m. that night, someone accidentally knocked at our door. I quickly gave a sign to Lucky to just keep quiet, and luckily, Lucky understood!

What a close call!

Three months after that trip, Lucky died of some heart complications following the surgical removal of the kidney stones. He was 8.5 years old. Since we often travel, while we are still young enough and healthy enough at this time, we decided to do without the company of a dog for the time being. Perhaps in later years…

After almost two years of having a very lucrative return from the duplex, about 10% NOI (Net Operating Income), I had saved enough money to purchase another duplex, around the same area as our townhome (i.e. Clearwater, Florida).

We found yet another one fairly easily. Kevin was so thrilled about this one. I asked him to use his trading money to help me finance the purchase, but he was somewhat reluctant. I carried on with the process of the purchase, such as making an offer, having it accepted, and then giving the deposit cheque and getting the inspection done by a home Inspector. At the same time, I also monitored Kevin's demeanor to see, whether he would chip in with the payment for this investment.

During the inspection, it was very clear to me that he was not going to use his money at all.

I was quite disappointed and decided to back off the purchase altogether. This decision was facilitated by the rudeness of the listing agent. Although I had spent $450.00 USD for the home Inspector, my mind was definitely made up to cancel the transaction. It felt like a whisper from my guardian angel initially, and the whisper was amplified by Kevin's uncooperative behavior, and loudest still by the realtor's rudeness. This turned out to be my saving grace for "The BEST is yet to COME!" (I.e., another home away from home, this time in Vancouver!).

In Chapter 12, I will describe my experience with Vancouver's purchases.

The lesson from the above incident, was, to never waiver in participating proactively all the time.

When things seem to turn out to be unpleasant, just be brave enough to cut your losses, instead of stubbornly following the original plan. Always go with the flow of your heart's desire. You can never go wrong! Be bold, but in moderation. Think, reflect on what could happen if you carry on, and if you stop. Write the pros and the cons on the piece of paper. Pray/ meditate on the situation, so that you may be given clarity, as to what you should do. Very often for me, the clear answer comes in the morning, after my refreshing sleep, or after my rosary prayer.

OFFER ON MY FLORIDA HOME

Although we loved our 2-bedroom townhome in Florida very much, somehow after 5 years of owning it, I was feeling that the time had come to try to sell the present one and replace it with a detached house instead. For the last 2 years, I had been getting a regular renter— a couple of retired teachers from Michigan—for periods of 6 months. They are true snowbirds, enjoying the warm weather during the winter. They come on November 1st and leave April 30th.

A few months ago, when I was dog sitting in Florida for Angie's 2 dogs, just before Christmas 2019, I told the renters of our home away from home, about my plan to sell the townhome, and I said that I would give them the first right of refusal. They told me that they would think about this offer and would get back to me in a few days' time. Two days later, they asked us to come over to discuss it. We stopped by at the appointed time. They were ready to buy! We discussed the terms and the price. After that, we increased our efforts in trying to find another property to be our home away from home. The market was so overheated at that time. Four days went by, and we still could not locate our replacement property. Kevin was very worried that he would not find one he liked, as he had already been very happy with the present townhome. To allay his anxieties, I had to tone down my very different feeling in this matter.

I felt confident that a detached home would not be too hard to find. Moving up is always easier than downsizing. Reluctantly, I phoned Greg, the tenant, and told him that we needed to make the transaction conditional on us acquiring a new property. An hour later, he phoned back to tell us that he would increase the purchase price by $10,000 USD.

For the sake of keeping harmony in our marriage, with a heavy heart, I had to say no to Greg. Deep down in my heart, with this decision, I felt that somehow "the BEST is yet to COME."

Time will tell!

September 15/2020: I am happy to share that my compromise with Kevin was indeed the right way! Covid-

19 has attacked the whole planet earth since early March for us in Canada. We had planned to use our Clearwater, Florida home away from home in May to search for a newer and better place than the present one. With the current situation, we are delaying the plan until the vaccine is available to control the spread of the corona virus. Greg will also stay put in Michigan for this coming winter. In the meantime, I am keeping myself occupied with the marketing of this book and other interesting shows on TV, a daily brisk walk for 30 minutes, plus lots of readings to satisfy my intellectual need.

SMOOTH SALE OF MY CONDO

As soon as we were back in Toronto, I asked a very dear friend of ours if he wanted to purchase a bachelor condo with an excellent long-term tenant. I offered one year free management for them.

The husband was somewhat interested and asked for an appointment. FORTUNATELY, his wife did not agree with the investment idea. I'll tell you in the next paragraph why I said "fortunately."

Prior to this, I tried to sell the property to the tenant. Again, FORTUNATELY, he was not qualified to purchase. Strangely, somehow I was meant to experience (and to share this experience with you) that selling property can indeed feel like selling peanuts.

I listed this condo for $3,000.00 more than the price I had offered to the tenant and our good friend. Within two days, I had 7 offers, and it then was sold for $40,000.00 more than the offer I had made to the two candidates as mentioned above; and my promise to the present tenant was kept, he did not have to move out.

All four parties, the buyer and her realtor, the tenant, and I were all very pleased with the outcome. This was one of my successful transactions, whereby all parties experience the benefit, WIN for ALL!!

PARTICIPATION IN LIFE

Now with the Covid-19 situation, I am using this social distancing time to concentrate on finishing my book much sooner than it otherwise would have been. This pandemic of the Coronavirus has been affecting all facets of everyone's lives in an unprecedented way. Kevin was supposed to see his mother in Jakarta, on March 3, 2020.

Thanks to the flooding of the area close to his mother's house, just 10 days prior to leaving Toronto, he decided to cancel the trip. I am very grateful about this. Without the flood, he would have proceeded with the trip, and might have been afflicted or become a carrier unknowingly. Both were avoided in the nick of time. What a gift from heaven!

If we keep on giving feedback and acknowledgement

each time, we will be frequently rewarded. Participating fully in your own situations is highly recommended if you want to create a satisfying life.

I can recall an amazing phenomenon from a few years ago, when Kevin had just returned from Jakarta.

I was just looking randomly at his emails, from behind his back, with him being aware of what I was doing. Suddenly, I zeroed in on a particular email address, and my heart palpitated wildly for some unknown reason. I was given a premonition!

I thought he must have been corresponding with this former classmate that he had had a crush on during his teenage years.

And yes, it turned out to be true. There was also a telephone call he made at about 1:30 a.m., when he thought I was asleep. Good job the long distance between Toronto and Jakarta made it impossible for that attraction to become fatal. I was fully engaged and aware about all those and more…

The fact of the matter was that I was very much challenged in the last twenty years or so. My career as an entrepreneur has been very interesting indeed. I thoroughly enjoyed my tasks in helping people obtain their principal residences as well as their investments. Alongside them, I was also busy with procuring my very own portfolios in properties. My challenges came from my marital instabilities, due to many trials and tribulations that life threw at us, some of which I am sharing with you here. Through my positive outlook on life, and most importantly, by the grace of our good Lord, I can say that for the most part, I am happy and hopeful.

One time when I was about to go out, I had a strange premonition, that Kevin was about to call his former client (whom I knew to be a bit of a flirt), to wish her a happy birthday. When I came home, I immediately dialed the last number called. It was a "gotcha" moment!! I treasure this gift that appears once in a while in my life. I would say, that my guardian angels were the ones guiding me through all the aspects of my spiritual experiences. I am happy to participate fully in the physical, mental, and spiritual aspects of my life.

We all experience our own trials and tribulations all the time, right? Through them all we become the resilient people we are meant to be. Just hang in there—the BEST is yet to COME! Enjoy the journey and the process, for life is what we make it out to be. The choice is all yours, whether it's going to be heaven on earth, or hell on earth. Your mind is powerful; use it wisely, joyfully.

I was ordained to learn my life lessons by the fact that my husband would often be impatient and unduly critical. He seemed to indicate that his being right was better than our being happy. Although I know for 100%, that this thought was totally misguided, and I would not engage in this kind of conflict, to date, I have not quite mastered this challenge yet. I still need to explore the peaceful ways to harmonize the situation I am in.

Instead of feeling down and discouraged, I bounced back each time I saw it coming my way. In itself, this doesn't amount to perfecting the transcendence I desire for both of us as couple. When, in the near future, the moment I could feel that he has transformed himself to be at peace with our achievements together……,this would be gigantic!
Or, the moment I could feel peaceful with whatever situation I am in, this would also be….gigantic! The BEST is yet to COME!

My belief is to be always on the lookout to transform all the challenges to shape/mold me to be the best person I can be. As long as I am better today than yesterday, I am happy and contented. By this mindset, I manage to feel excited in the face of CALAMITIES ... for they are steps to help me reach my Divine DESTINY.

THE REWARD FOR HELPING OTHERS

During Angie's medical schooling in Saba Island, my real estate business was exceptional. Clients called me in droves constantly. Each year, Angie asked me if she needed to take a post graduate student loan, as I asked her to always check that with me. And each time, I am happy to share here, I could reassure her that I was able to handle the cost for the following year.

The moment she was working and earning pretty well in Canton as a resident in the family practice, my business took a nosedive. By this time, I had my passive income established and, therefore, I was spared from this decreased commission and could live well without a care in the world. This happened by design and not by chance. It was just like during the start of my early days as a realtor, when I found it annoying to NOT be able to use my money at all. Kevin was using our joint account to feed his trading in the stock market. This was a very huge stickler for years in our marriage. It was resolved automatically as God helped me by showing that I did not have to worry about money. I just had to concentrate on my good service to people in my capacity as a broker in my real estate business, and the money would flow as a byproduct. Some realtors are too money minded, and the clients can feel it, and they subsequently run away.

ALWAYS READY TO HELP

As another example of helping others, I was rewarded by some unexpected blessings, much greater than anything I could imagine. The real story, I am sharing here:

One day, Fran, my previous client, whose English was

not so good, approached me to help her evict her tenant. She had a professional tenant from hell, who had not paid neither his rent for 6 months, nor his utilities. I knew that I would need to take this tenant to court for sure, and a sheriff would be needed to enforce this eviction. Common sense told me that all the compensation I would get, would definitely not be worth it. My time, plus the frustration I would face, were just too painful to imagine, but I could not refuse her request either. She had given me many transactions over the years. With a heavy heart, I took on this challenge.

The procedures were indeed lengthy, frustrating, and complicated. I even had to delay my road trip, from Toronto to Florida by two days, and made long distance calls from Florida to the court's clerk in Toronto.

It must have taken me about three months before the Sheriff could be employed to get the tenant out. I had to deal with the tenant myself during the initial stage. He appeared unkempt, and the rented house was very dirty. On top of that, he kept a big dog. My strategy was to put a FOR SALE sign outside the house, with EXCLUSIVE written on it. By "exclusive," I mean that the house could only be sold through my Company. Fran did not really want to sell her house at this time. It really required a massive repair work. Her tenant had ruined her property extensively.

I called the tenant for the showing of the house, and in

my mind, he would do some cleaning as per my request. I would give him one or even two days' notice. Verbally, he seemed cooperative, but when it comes to the day of appointment, he let me down twice. Both times, he agreed, but then he wouldn't answer when I knocked at the door. Although I had the key, I could not go in, as the big dog would bark, and I would be foolish to take any chance to go inside.

Now, the handsome reward from doing the above undertaking came from an Indonesian couple, who called me and wanted to see the house but could not get in. I got to know Don and Karen, very well during the meeting. I had a very good feeling about them, and this feeling must have been reciprocated by them. They told me that ideally they would rent for one year, and then buy the following year. Since we were not able to see the house, I showed them some houses for rent with a stipulation to buy after the one-year lease.

By the third showing, Don and Karen were happy to have found a house they liked. I put an offer in for them, with the purchase price agreed upon twelve months down the road.

After nine months elapsed, I did a preapproval through my trusted mortgage broker. Don liked to handle the paperwork by himself, and I respected that.

He had experienced a purchase of a house out of

Ontario; hence, I did not insist on him to deal with my contact. It was only fair to let him decide who he wanted to use for his mortgage need.

I was not privy as to what mortgage company he chose to handle his application for a mortgage.

Just three weeks prior to closing date, it was lucky for them, that they voiced their concerns about how they suspected a conspiracy among the seller, his chosen mortgage broker (he chose the seller's mortgage broker instead of the one I referred him to), and the lawyer. Both the lawyer and the mortgage broker were the seller's recommendations. I put a call in to the mortgage broker and the lawyer, and I asked for the progress, plus the commitment of the mortgage approval.

I did not get the commitment in writing at all, only verbally.

I started to find alternative financing from some private lenders. At that time, the demand for properties was by far exceeding the supply. The price increase, by day, was ridiculous. The seller purposely wanted Don and Karen to back out of the purchase. Luckily the house was destined to be for them. That's why they involved me at the crucial time prior to the closing. I did tell them that creative financing had been my niche in my present profession since I started over twenty years ago. Good job they remembered that.

They involved me to get the new approval and the new lawyer until they managed to close their first purchase in Toronto.

Without helping Fran with her big headache of getting rid of her awful tenant, I would not have met Don and Karen. They are nice people to get to know, and I was very pleased to be able to facilitate the transaction that was almost nullified by the unscrupulous conspiracy of the seller and his cronies.

What a nice memory to be able to act swiftly in time, for Don, Karen, and myself included.

When the going gets tough, the tough gets going. It's very true if you believe it. When I feel very overwhelmed, I have been training myself to totally surrender. To let go and let God. It has been my modus operandi since I was jilted years ago. At that time, after a deep reflection and postulate, I had slept so soundly for twelve hours. I had felt so incredulous about the absurdities of how it could happen to me. Of course, this does happen, time and time and time again, to so many people! I was naïve to have thought that I would have been spared from this "slap" on my face. In hindsight, I handled the humiliation pretty well, and got up super fast, followed by a mature resolve.

We need to frequently remind ourselves to always get up each time we fall on our face...

Chapter 12

Investments in Vancouver

"Motivation is the art of getting people to do what you want them to do because they want to do it." Dwight Eisenhower

Motivating people with the above thought requires a lot of practice. Once you master it, your life will be just incredibly easy. Some charismatic leaders and teachers possess this exceptional talent.

I have always enjoyed my hot bath prior to my bed time. This helps me to unwind, and relax, and hence a good sleep will ensue. As my work is kind of sedentary, I also use the hot bath to stretch my muscles. I would lie down on my stomach and stretch my legs with the exaggerated movement of bringing my knees up alternately. It has helped me a great deal with my backaches. Once or twice, I needed to compress my back with Zheng Gu Shui.

Most of the time, I just manage/prevent the backache from manifesting itself by my stretches in the bathtub. I would spend half to one hour every night on what is totally "Me" time. I even "heard a whisper" during this quiet time. It was indeed strange that, mysteriously and very suddenly, I was nudged to check on some papers under the table in my office. I found Kevin's papers, with written instructions to our accountant, to keep his stock market's loss strictly confidential.

Kevin had been guarding his papers very carefully, so that they would not be seen by me. I was mystically guided to that place by my guardian angels. The practice of hiding this fact did not sit well with me.

Transparency in a marriage is crucial. I had to steady myself and get a good grip on myself, instead of going into battle after the revelation of Kevin's loss in his trading. This required a lot of self-control, and I am happy to say that I managed to conquer my desire to confront the situation head on. With every heated situation such as this, I often concentrate on my breathing, and I play the scenario in my head.

If I do the right thing, in accordance with what my purpose is, in living and breathing on this earth, my loving God will definitely approve of my self-control and my intention to live in harmony.

He will be the ONE to show me that the result will be just magnificent. When God is on my side, no one and nothing can put me in harm's way. Subconsciously, it's not hard to nail it with certainty of what choice one should take. Every one of us is given the freedom to decide what to choose. The moment you decide to follow your kindhearted instincts in the situation you are in, the easier it is to take your stand.

I can always feel God's approval when I choose something that is not easy for me to do, but benefits someone else a great deal. Just see your result after the fact. If your result is good, next time you will be more inclined to listen to the little kind voice from your heart.

Reflecting quietly and comfortably while soaking in the nice hot bath, is spiritually inspiring; or soaking myself in the feelings of gratitude for all the blessings I have received, and am about to receive. I treasure this time very much! The time to unwind from the hectic day, to prepare for some restful sleep with pleasant dreams.

THE POWER OF PRAYERS

Daily rosary prayers have been another amazingly blessed spiritual activity for me. I started this ritual after my pilgrimage to Guadalupe, Mexico, for 7 days, from November 9, 2011. It was quite a surprise to me how Kevin, (who had indicated his dislikes in joining any pilgrimage) wanted to join a pilgrimage—the very first one! The second pilgrimage was to Lourdes in France, in 2016; and the third was to pray through Padre Pio in Italy, and then Lourdes again, and Fatima in Portugal, in October 2019.

I am intrigued whenever I reflect on those phenomenal trips he so willingly took with me. How could those be possible?? Life is indeed an enigma. Whenever I aim for the greater good, I am humbled by many events that bring me down to my knees by "how great Thou art."

Annmarie had never wanted to be a nurse as her career, but now she is one, and she's pretty happy doing it.

When she graduated as a BScN, she approached me to ask my opinion if she could study pharmacy in England. I asked her to give the nursing career two years before trying to study undergraduate again.

Prior to her nursing study, she did four years undergraduate in psychology and political science. She obtained her first B.A. Honors degree. So, now, with two Bachelors' degree, it was really time for her to earn a living at this time. Otherwise, she might just keep on studying for the fun of it, and that would lead her to be reluctant to contribute her fair share to the society.

Whatever we decide, there will be a list of advantages and disadvantages. The main advantage of being a nurse is the ability to get a job very easily, post-graduation. It is also easy to find another job when you move to another city/province/country and last but not least, if she needs to work after her childbirth, (if/when she is ready), it is quite easy to find a part-time job with short working hours per day.

Thankfully, she listened. After two years, she got to like the profession.

When Annmarie was 19 years of age, in her first year at the University of Toronto, she asked me how she would know which man to marry. I just said: "You will just know it, but you need to let time tell and not to rush it."

Although she did have a few guys who were interested in her, she did not have any interest in pursuing an exclusive relationship until she met her future husband.

By that time, we asked her to join us to go to Bali Island in Indonesia, as well as visiting relatives in Jakarta, especially her paternal grandmother. We felt, that before she would be married, the timing was perfect to vacation together as a family. For just over 2 weeks, we really enjoyed our family time together. The only thing that spoiled our family vacation was the diarrhea that Annmarie and I suffered on the second day we were in Jakarta, for about three days. Luckily, all three of us were at the peak of our health when we were in Bali. From Toronto, we landed in Bali and had a marvelous time being driven around for three days by a local driver that I had booked from Toronto, from 9 a.m. till about 8 p.m.

True to our instincts, after about a year of courtship, Annmarie got engaged, moved to Vancouver, and married 18 months later. They got married at a beautiful resort on Vancouver Island. For a late October wedding, the weather was quite warm and sunny. My high hope was that this marriage would be as wonderful as the weather was on that momentous day, and that the unusually bright and warm day, would be a good sign from above!

Prior to the wedding, Angie, Kevin, and I stayed in Vancouver, in May, to help out with some of the things needed for Annmarie's wedding. They only planned to have immediate family and close friends to witness them tying the knot. We totally agreed that it was wise not to have a big (and often meaningless) party for her very important milestone.

During this time, Kevin and I went to a local real estate brokerage and discussed our plan to find a home away from home that would include everything, so that we could just bring our clothes to live there. The realtor told us that it was highly unlikely to find such a place, but that she would try her best to keep an eye out for it. She prepared for us to go forward to look at some properties within our price range anyway.

Investments in Vancouver

We did see nine properties within the next three days. None caught our interest, till, excitedly, our realtor asked me to meet her in the lobby of a four-story building. This 1-bedroom unit was on the fourth floor, the very top floor/penthouse unit, overlooking a beautiful mountain view. The BEST part was, the seller was relocating to another province and would prefer to sell all the contents to the buyer, at the right price. We eagerly went to see the unit, and loved it! Immediately, I instructed Diane, the realtor, to write an offer. With the current technology, I could initial and sign the offer electronically. She called me prior to her emailing the offer, with the not so good news that, I had to compete with another prospective buyer. Hence, I had to use my gut feeling to know, how much more money I needed to offer, over and above the asking price.

After discussing the strategy with Diane, I offered $30,000.00 above the asking price, with all the unit's contents, such as the appliances, furniture, dinnerware, cookware, linens, etc.

An hour later, Diane asked me to improve my offer. I asked her to add $5,000.00, with the message not to lose this deal, meaning that she needed to get back to me again for more, if the $5,000.00 was not enough to secure the purchase. Half an hour later, Diane happily informed me that my offer was accepted. Wow, I was very excited and grateful with this outcome. Yippee...

Let me retrace my steps to the time that I cancelled my purchase of a duplex, due to my husband's refusal to chip in some money, coupled with the listing agent's rudeness during the home inspection.

At that time, based on my gut feeling, I just bowed out. That turned out to be very appropriate, as the money for that duplex, could conveniently be used for this lovely unit. It is in Port Coquitlam, within a half an hour drive from Vancouver. You see, by thinking positively, and focusing on imagining that I would be able to find a home away (in or near Vancouver) from my home in Toronto, I did get a rare deal. It happened just within one week after my meeting with the realtor in her office. Angie was still in Vancouver, too. We were at the airport when I heard the good news that my offer was accepted. We celebrated this joyous occasion very happily and gratefully. The closing date was pretty close to Annmarie's wedding in October.

My positive thinking and mental visualization worked well again. The anticipation of my projected wish to own another home away from home had just materialized. I managed to postulate…again!!

Note: postulate means self-created truth by thinking it, saying it, or writing it down.

I was feeling much more relaxed, compared with my first purchase of my "home away from home" in

Clearwater, Florida. I also planned to rent the unit during the months I would be away from Port Coquitlam.

After Annmarie's wedding, I emphasized to both of the newlyweds that she needed to get a car. A few months went by, and still no car for her. I booked a flight to see her on April 25, 2018, 6 months after the October wedding. I said to her on the phone, in mid-April: "On April 28th, your Dad and I will help you choose a car, so that you can practise driving comfortably. Okay?" That was what we did precisely. How did I do that? Remember, I am in the habit of acknowledging and appreciating any postulate that comes my way…

My positive disposition urges me to manifest my self-created truth in the physical world. It is fun and exciting to have this ability. So, when it feels right, I verbalize my hunch right away. It manifests faster and faster, too. When you belief this phenomenon, you, too, can do this.

My mantra of ORA (pray) et LABORA (labour/effort) facilitates my visions, too. They appear in the physical world by design and not by chance! The results of my postulates never cease to amaze me, that, I am able to "WILL" certain things to come into being, wow! It is awesome, indeed!

Focus on your good goal, and you will attract that into your physical world. Always acknowledge it gratefully and gracefully. Keep trying and have fun with it. You will be so happy you did...

On our next visit, early May 2019, Kevin and I were back in Port Coquitlam. During our chats with Annmarie, we came to know that Dan (Annmarie's husband) thought it was high time to start a family. He was ready, but Annmarie was not. He said that if she would not cooperate, they should get a divorce. Upon hearing this, Kevin and I were very upset. We decided to purchase a 1-bedroom unit in Vancouver, for her to just have her very own place, before he threatens her again.

We searched some websites and made appointments to see the properties. On the fifth day of our search, on Saturday, we went to some open houses. We really loved one of them. An offer was prepared by Susan, the realtor who attended the open house. She happened to be a Chinese Canadian from Indonesia. This was a good coincidence, plus, Susan is very pleasant and delightful to deal with, an essential factor to have in procuring any property.

After negotiating back and forth in the evening, we got it in the early hours of the morning, (i.e. at 00:30 a.m.) Sunday morning. What a relief...The closing date was set to be in two weeks' time. We had to postpone our flight back to Toronto.

Investments in Vancouver

After my first experience of buying a home away from home in Florida, this time, in Vancouver, I was even more sure that my postulate would be swift!

I should be able to find tenants (for the duration of a minimum of 30 days for each booking). My main concern was the cleaning person and handyman. As for the key, Kevin could very easily install a lock that could be opened using combination numbers. For a high-rise building, I would need someone who lives nearby to keep the fob to open the front door.

All the concerns were not that hard to overcome. Do you know why? It's simply due to the fact that as a positive person, I BELIEVE in all the help I would get. When I believe, I will always SEE, as long as the intention is for the greater good and for the service of others.

True to my expectation, it was easy to find tenants in both Florida and B.C. (British Columbia, Canada). All the support persons I needed just appeared one by one through some referrals. Again, I am emphasizing here: not by chance, but by design! When I need something right away, I seek and I always find; not to mention that I will think, contemplate, and pray prior to the undertakings, then move forward with all my might. Usually the process would be smooth, and if there should be any persistent resistance at all, I would stop and readjust my goal. It sounds very simple, right? In practice, initially, each effort can be quite daunting. Only with constant practice and discipline, it will get simpler and satisfying.

Conclusion

For me, it has been quite enjoyable recalling the positives in my life. Now, allow me to reiterate my purpose of writing this book. It is my hope, that, after digesting my stories, you can adopt:

1) My positive thinking. Life is indeed much more interesting when you are upbeat and full of hope. Be an OPTIMIST. Develop your sense of humor.

2) The willingness to help others around you, see for yourself, and prove my points; it will also give great rewards to you.

3) Postulates (self created truth by thinking it, saying it, or writing it down). The moment you succeed in doing one, you need to acknowledge it gratefully and gracefully, to attract the next one, then the next one! It's indeed amazing!!

4) The ability to always anticipate/think of possible good outcomes. These will follow after each trial/ tribulation. The BEST is yet to COME! Overcome your obstacles by

busying yourself doing SOME things instead of being consumed by anxiety/ paralyzed by doing nothing.

5) The more you give good service cheerfully, the more money will chase after you.

6) The attitude of gratitude. The endorphins or feel-good hormones will be produced without any rigorous physical exercises needed. The power of your mind is in need of being acknowledged and applied right now. Smile and laugh heartily often, and these will also make your body produce endorphins. Stay away from experimenting with any alcoholic drinks, recreational drugs, and other things that can lead to addiction, such as gambling, in the casinos or "intellectually," such as in daily online trading. Once the addiction takes hold on you, it will make you oblivious to everything else. Please establish only positive habits that will uplift you...

7) We all are spiritual beings experiencing physical trials and tribulations, to complete our individual transcendence.

From my many testimonies that I shared with you in this book, you may be able to add the number of benefits for yourself. Apply all of the law of the Universe that you know of. Hence, always think good things, say good things, and do good things.

Conclusion

Life is sacred...Appreciate it, enjoy it, and make the BEST of it! We are all in it together. Be kind, always!

www.ingramcontent.com/pod-product-compliance
Lightning Source LLC
Chambersburg PA
CBHW071119090426
42736CB00012B/1957